History of the Knights of Pythias

Also from Westphalia Press

westphaliapress.org

History of the Knights of Pythias

by Jos D. Weeks

WESTPHALIA PRESS
An imprint of Policy Studies Organization

Westphalia Press
An imprint of Policy Studies Organization
1527 New Hampshire Ave., NW
Washington, D.C. 20036
info@ipsonet.org

ISBN-13: 978-1941755921
ISBN-10: 1941755925

Cover design by Taillefer Long at Illuminated Stories:
www.illuminatedstories.com

Daniel Gutierrez-Sandoval, Executive Director
PSO and Westphalia Press

Devin Proctor, Director of Media and Publications
PSO and Westphalia Press

Updated material and comments on this edition
can be found at the Westphalia Press website:
www.westphaliapress.org

HISTORY

OF THE

KNIGHTS OF PYTHIAS,

WITH AN

ACCOUNT OF THE LIFE AND TIMES

OF

DAMON AND PYTHIAS.

BY

JOS. D. WEEKS, A. B.

THIRD EDITION.

CINCINNATI:

J. HALE POWERS & CO.,

FRATERNITY PUBLISHERS.

1872.

To the

Supreme Lodge of the World,

KNIGHTS OF PYTHIAS.

PREFACE.

T has not been our aim in this little volume simply to repeat the story of the friendship of Damon and Pythias. Had it been, much time and labor might have been spared by telling it. But we have endeavored to show what it was that led them, even in the face of death, to be true to each other. This we believe to have been the teachings of the Pythagorean Society. In carrying out our purpose, we have not only given an account of the life of Pythagoras, and of the constitution of his society, but of the three other great Secret Societies of antiquity, the Eleusinian, the Isianic, and the Cabirian, which had such an influence upon Pythagoras and his society.

The rapid spread of our Order, and the constant inquiries concerning its history and principles, demand that every true Knight be ready, for the honor of our institution, to explain the latter and tell the former. To aid in this duty, and at the same time to make the hidden meanings of our beautiful Ritual plain, has been our object. How far we have succeeded, we leave to the judgment of every intelligent Knight.

Our thanks are due to those brethren who have so kindly furnished us accounts of the rise of the Order in the States. We have also laid under contribution the Supreme and Grand Lodge Reports, and especially Bro. Shackleford's KNIGHT'S ARMOR.

CINCINNATI, *January* 10, 1871.

CONTENTS.

7

CHAPTER IV.

CHAPTER V.

CHAPTER VI.

CHAPTER VII.

CHAPTER VIII.

PART II.

History of the Knights of Pythias.

CHAPTER IX.

CHAPTER X.

CHAPTER XI.

CHAPTER XII.

CHAPTER XIII.

PART I.

Life and Times of Damon and Pythias.

Chapter I.

The Origin and Development of the Secret Societies of Greece.

OR three thousand years now, Secret Societies have existed in the world. How far back of this their history reaches, it is impossible to state, but it would not be too much to assert that they must have had an origin coeval with that of human society. As the nations of antiquity have emerged from the darkness of traditional history, ever in the forefront of their progress has marched some Secret Society or Mystery. Gathered within these were earnest men, who saw beneath the shows of things, and had the eye to read and the courage to believe THE TRUTH. To be sure, they were few who thus saw. There were not many who dared lift the veil that hid the face of Isis from the vulgar gaze, but in this they

differed not much from the way of the world. When
new elements are to be sent forth into the world,
when new evangels are to be preached, or new de-
partures of humanity to be made, it is only here and
there one goes on the mission or does the work. So
it has ever been, so will it ever be. Humanity
never rises in the mass. It straggles onward, a few
in the van bearing the brunt of the fight, while the
great army follows after, and often a long way after.

These Societies have been of incalculable benefit
to man. In the earliest days of the world, the
wisest and best of men sought in their secret temples to penetrate the mysterious gloom which en-
shrouded, not only their own being, but God as well.

They toiled in labor and pain, baffled often and
oft losing their way, but there was an earnestness
in their attempt which ennobled them. Nor did
they labor in vain, as we shall have occasion to
show. Some idea of a true God and a true life
they found. One they worshiped, the other they
lived. The ideal formed they tried to put into their
lives, and here, again, the attempt was not wholly
fruitless. Osiris and Isis, Eleusis, the Cabiri, Pythagoras, Odin, are names that have not been without their influence on the world. We can not
correctly understand the history of the nations of

antiquity, much less their theology, philosophy, science, or ethics, without a knowledge of these Societies. In a word, out of these has been evolved civilization. Some of the grandest ideas, those which have had the greatest influence on human progress, were born amid the mystic symbols.

Nor has an advancing civilization, under new conditions, and with new truths as its basis, taught us to do without these Societies. To-day many of the highest and holiest principles of true religion receive their most perfect exemplification in the Secret Societies. It is a fact, one in view of which the Church of to-day should hide its head in shame, that the great idea of the brotherhood of man must look to these institutions for its most perfect development. Seeing this to be so, men are every year crowding their doors; millions of earth's best and truest men, its kings and rulers, its sages and statesmen, and the priests of our holy religion, gather in every clime about the altars of the different Fraternities, and listen obediently to the clink of the gavel.

The subject of the history and principles of these Societies has not received attention commensurate with its importance. A few take the trouble to look up the history of the Order to which they individually belong, and here their labors end. The number is exceedingly small who go further, and strive to learn the relation that exists between their Fraternity and others, and the principles underlying and sustaining the union. Such is the task, however, we have proposed to ourselves—an endeavor to connect the history of the youngest secret society of the world with some of the oldest—to take the child of but yesterday and lead him to the hoary patriarch of the old days, to learn what his wisdom may reveal.

In this attempt to tell the history of the Knights of Pythias, and show the reasons of their success, it can not be foreign to our purpose to trace the origin and development of Secret Societies in general.

And we premise that we are of that class who believe that the original state of man was in society—that he is, by nature, a social being, and delights in the companionship of his fellow. We grant, of course, that to-day the world is filled with envy and hatred—that men are isolated, turned against each other, clutching what each can get, and calling it "mine." We own, further, that to many, friendship and communion are only names—that home, the sacred foundation of society, is to thousands on this plodding earth only a place in which to eat and sleep—a sort of human stable. Yet this very envy and hatred of men only proves our position. Carlyle has put this whole argument in a single question. He asks, "Were I a steam-engine, wouldst thou take the trouble to tell lies of me? Not thou! I should grind on, all unheeded, whether badly or well."[1]

If here it is asked, If this be so, if communion, if society be by nature the state of man, why is there so much disunion, and strife, and selfishness? why, instead of human helpfulness and kindness, were there, in the ancient days, so much hate and hindering? the answer is simple: These things existed for the same reason that society is disorganized to-day, because men will sin; in a word, it is crime that has disorganized society. And this is not alone the teaching of that old Hebrew Book, but it is the universal testimony and belief of every religion of the world. The Grecian mythology teaches the same truth. All was peace and harmony until guilt entered, and then war began. After Mother Earth had sprung forth from Chaos, the first-born was Eros (Love), the subduer of gods and men, and her reign continued until crime came. When Kronos would slay his father and spilled his

[1] Sartor Resartus, III, vii.

2

blood, it was from this blood that the Erinnys, the Furies, sprung.[2]

With this crime, and its consequent idea of guilt, came also the feeling of the necessity of some way to regain what was lost.   In other words, man felt the necessity of a purification and an atonement.   This could not be found in the ordinary worship, for that was for man while in a state of innocency, and as a stain of guilt had fallen, some special means was necessary.   In cases of involuntary homicide, this was especially imperative.   The guilty person was thought unfit for the society of men and the worship of the gods, until he was free from the taint of blood.   For this purpose certain ceremonies were instituted.

Here was the origin of Secret Societies, or the Mysteries of Greece.   They were adjuncts of religion, celebrated in honor of some particular god, entirely separate from the ordinary worship, and designed to meet cases that the usual ceremonials of religion could not satisfy.   These Mysteries were celebrated apart from the citizens generally, and approachable only through a certain course of preparation and initiation, and were even forbidden to be talked of in presence of the uninitiated, under

[2] Hesiod Theog., 116 et passim.

the severest threats of Divine judgment. Æschylus, only suspected of revealing them, was forced to take sanctuary for his life at the altar of Bacchus, until he had an opportunity of appealing to Areopagus.

Though we have taken homicide as an example, it must not be supposed that it was only in cases of this crime that the Greeks regarded purification necessary. The greatest use of the mysteries was in times of general distress and danger, disease, public calamity, or religious terror and despondency. Men were then prone to believe that what they were suffering arose from the displeasure of the gods, and as they found that the ordinary sacrifices and worship were insufficient for their protection, they eagerly made use of these Mysteries, thinking that in these a purer and holier worship and oblation might be offered.

The most celebrated of these special rites in the Pan-Hellenic world were those of the Idean Zeus, in Crete; of Demeter, at Eleusis; of the Cabiri, in Samothrace, and Dionysius, at Delphi and Thebes.

Such, then, was the origin of the Grecian Mysteries. They had their birth in a deep-felt need of a higher and holier worship than was found about the daily altars and in the common sacrifices. They were the answers given to the craving of the Greek mind for a more intimate communion with its gods—a craving that came from a sense of the Divine displeasure, we own; but is it not always true that it is the heart that feels most deeply its guilt whose cries are loudest for its God?

Keeping this origin in mind, the development may easily be traced. Seeing that in the hour of their extreme need, help came to them through the prayers of the Hierophants of these Mysteries, they began to look upon them, not simply as something for occasional use, but as having higher ideas of Deity, and as exerting, through their peculiar holiness, a greater influence with the gods. The priests of these Mysteries, without any design to impose upon the multitude, could readily have believed all this, and willingly imparted to those who came, the story of how the gods had aided those who approached the shrine. At first, it might have been told simply as a tale of the beneficence of the Deity, but in course of time solemn preliminaries were introduced, to prepare the candidate, and scenic representations, to force home on his mind the story. These joined with religious instruction, we have as a result the Mystery, in its highest development.

What these particular representations were, and what special religious doctrines were advanced in each, will appear in the course of our work. There were, however, some things common to them all that may be spoken of here. It is very certain that the true teachings of the Mysteries were of a higher moral tone than was generally prevalent in the world. The great doctrine of Divine Providence, to which each is debtor, and under whose dominion each exists, seems to have been the first impressed upon the mind of the initiate. To this were joined the ideas of the omnipresence and omniscience of God, the belief in the immortality of the soul, the necessity of an upright, holy life, enforced by the idea of future rewards and punishments. In inculcating these doctrines, especially that of a future life, it was taught that the initiated would be happier in that state than all other mortals; that while the souls of the profane, upon leaving their bodies, stuck fast in mire and filth and dwelt in darkness, the souls of the initiated winged their flight directly to the happy islands and the habitations of the gods. Socrates says of them, "In my opinion, those who established the Mysteries—whoever they were—were well skilled in human nature. For, in these rites, it was of old signified to the aspirant, that those who died without being initiated stuck fast in mire and filth, but that he who was purified and initiated, at his death should have his habitation with the gods."[3]

The mistake must not be made, however, of supposing that the doctrine was advanced, that initiation alone, or any other means except a virtuous life, could entitle man to this degree of happiness. The Mysteries openly proclaimed it as their chief business to restore man's "soul to that state from whence it fell, as from its native seat of perfection."[4] No wonder that the superior advantages of the initiated, both here and hereafter, should make the Mysteries universally aspired to. Men, women, and children ran to be initiated, and the general feeling is well expressed by honest farmer Trygaeus, in the Pax of Aristophanes, "I must be initiated before I die."

The obligation the initiates were under to lead a pure and virtuous life explains why the first thing taught in the great Mysteries was the delusion of the common religion. The insuperable obstacle to a life of purity and holiness was the vicious example of the gods. "Ego homuncio hoc non facerem?"[5] (Could not I, a sorry fellow, be permitted to do this thing?) was the universal formula when one would give loose rein to his passions. But the initiate

---

[3] Plato's Phedo. [4] Plato. [5] Terrence Eun, III, v.

being once shown that the whole Olympus was only dead mortals, their example could no longer be pleaded in extenuation of his crimes.

Such were the Secret Societies or the Mysteries of Greece, as found by Pythagoras—simply the repository of religious truth of a higher character than the multitude were allowed to know. There was not, in any true sense of the word, a fraternity. No special bond of union existed among the members, except that which came from a secret shared. The true ideal of a fraternity was yet to be worked out. The world was yet to see the society which, while it taught all that the Mysteries did, and even a better and purer theogony, should also teach fraternity—that, while it told of God and the duties man owed to him, should not forget man and his duty to his fellow-man.

This was the work Pythagoras accomplished, and that most successfully. While he taught a better, a higher religion, he forgot not to inculcate the lessons of friendship. Monotheistic in his belief, when all around was polytheistic, he taught the omnipresence of God, the immortality of the soul, and the necessity of personal holiness, to qualify man for admission into the society of the gods. This was the religious part of his system—not these doctrines as received at the present day, but simply a better belief than was known before.

But his great virtue lay in the fact that he made these ideas effective in regulating the actions of man toward man. To how great a degree this was done, let the story of Damon and Pythias show. We can only say, if that age produced any thing more self-sacrificing and noble than this, we have yet to learn of it.

Chapter II.

The Eleusinian Mysteries.

I N pursuing our inquiries into the nature of the various Mysteries, in which Pythagoras was initiated, we shall speak first of those of Eleusis. In dignity, these hold the highest rank, equally imposing in their origin, their renown, and their results. Among the ancients, these were the only ones that were ever dignified with the name Mysteries. All others were nothing more originally than the expert legerdemain of barbarian jugglers or the tricks of skilled mountebanks. The Bacchic or Orphic Mysteries are of an entirely different character, and in their wild frenzy no more resemble the grave dignity of those of Ceres, than the unbridled force of savage life resembles the civilization of well disci-

plined society. As early as the time of Solon, the
great Athenian lawgiver, and even in the time of
Draco, laws were made for the due and regular
celebration of the Eleusinian Mysteries.[1]   They
were held in such estimation that in time, not only
all Greece proper, but all the world hastened to be
initiated. Tully says, " From the remotest regions,
men came to be initiated," while Aristides calls
Eleusis the common temple of the earth. Especially in Greece and among the Grecians, was initiation an affair of the highest importance. To
bear the narthex, and join the procession that
moved across the little river Cephissus, was an
honor eagerly sought. Even kings and princes
craved the honor of wearing the mystic cincture
of the order. It was scandalous not to be initiated, and however virtuous the person otherwise
appeared, he became suspicious to the people did
he refuse, as was the case with Socrates. Plato,
who had entered the penetralia, did not speak of
them without admiration, and Cicero says, " Nothing
is more excellent than the Mysteries which exalt
us from a rude and savage state to true humanity.
They initiate us into the true principles of life, for

[1] Porphyry and Andocides.

they teach us not only to live pleasantly, but to die with better hopes."[2]

As we shall show hereafter, these mysteries were divided into two rites, the less and great. Of these the less were only a preparatory purification for the greater, and might be communicated to all. While only those of pure Hellenic descent could claim initiation into the greater, all, Greeks and barbarians, might present themselves for this honor to the less. The reason of this appears to be that in the great Mysteries, certain truths were taught that it was not considered best the people should know. It seems that the first great truth taught those who were judged capable, was that their whole system of religion was a delusion.[3] Jupiter, Mercury, Bacchus, Venus, and the whole rabble of their licentious gods, were stripped of their pretensions and shown to be only dead mortals, subject to the same passions and infirmities. The fabulous gods thus dethroned, the Supreme Cause of all things took his place. In other words, the Aporrettæ, or secrets of the greater Mysteries, were these two—the detection of vulgar polytheism and the discovery of the doctrine of the Divine Unity.[4] Strange as this

---

[2] De Leg. II, 14. [3] Warburton, Div. Leg.

[4] Warburton, Div. Leg.

statement may seem, the student of history can not doubt its truth. Tully, and Cicero, and Plutarch, and scores of others, confirm this. The very name given those initiated into the great Mysteries proves it true. They were called Epoptes, those that see things as they are, instead of Mystæ, which means just the opposite.

So sacred where these Mysteries held and so jealously were they guarded that no penalty was too severe to be visited upon their betrayer. Death was the instant result, and even to the grave the impious wretch was followed. Over his remains a column was erected, on which was told the story of his crime and its punishment. Æschylus, the great tragic poet, suspected of having revealed some part of the mysteries, barely escaped with his life, and only by proving that he had never been initiated, while Aristotle, accused of imitating the sacrificial rite of Eleusis, was tried and banished.[5] The hints we get of the nature of these secrets, make us regret this jealous care the more. Were it possible to lift the veil which covers these Mysteries, we should see to the very heart of the religious development of the Greeks.

The institution of these Mysteries may be placed

[5] Diog. Laert.

about 1399 B. C., in the reign of Erectheus. A fragment of marble preserved at Oxford gives this as the date. As this was three hundred years prior to the reign of David in Jerusalem, and more than six hundred before the first Olympiad, the beginning of true Grecian history, some idea may be formed of their antiquity.

The best accounts agree in ascribing their origin to Ceres herself. The account as given in the Homeric hymn is as follows. Proserpine,[6] the daughter of Ceres, while gathering flowers in a meadow, had been seized by Pluto, god of the lower world, and borne to his dark and dismal abode. Jupiter, the king of the gods, who was also the father of the stolen maiden, had given his consent to the abduction, so that her cries to him for help were in vain. Her mother, who had heard the echo of her voice as the Nysian plain opened to receive Proserpine, hastened to find her. For nine days she wandered in vain. On the tenth, meeting Hecate, together they hastened to Sol, or the Sun, who revealed the place of her captivity, and added that she had been carried off with the consent of Jupiter. Ceres was smitten with anger

---

[6] I use the Latin, instead of the Greek terms, as being better known.

and despair. She left Olympus, the abode of the gods, and wandered on earth, in grief, and fasting till her form could not be known. In this condition she came to Eleusis, and while sitting at a well, in the garb of an old woman, was met by the daughter of Celeus, king of Eleusis, from whom she sought employment. Being discovered in the attempt to render the foster child intrusted to her care immortal, the goddess revealed her true character, commanded that the people of Eleusis erect a temple and altar to her on the hill above the fountain, and promised to prescribe the orgies they should perform.

This was speedily done, and Ceres took up her abode in it still angry and dwelling apart from the gods. Thus she remained for a whole year—a desperate and terrible year—in vain did the oxen draw the plow, and in vain was the barley-seed cast into the furrow—Ceres would not permit it to grow.[7] Jupiter tried in vain to conciliate her. She refused to return to Olympus, and to restore fertility to the earth, until she had seen her daughter again. At last the terrible king of gods and men was forced to yield. Mercury was sent to Erebus for Proserpine—Ceres received her again, the buried

---

[7] Demeter the Greek name of Ceres, signifies Mother Earth.

seed came up in abundance from the earth. She
returned to Olympus to dwell, but not till she had
instructed Celeus in the divine service and the
solemnities which she required to be celebrated in
her honor.[8] Thus began the venerable Mysteries
of Eleusis; and though we read it as pleasing
poetry, and see in the rape of Proserpine only the
seed-grain imbedded in the ground during the
Winter, and in her return to her mother, Ceres, the
Earth, only the joyful return of Spring, we must
remember that to the Eleusinians this was genuine
and sacred history. They as much believed in the
existence of Ceres and her daughter as in their
own, and with a corresponding reverence and earnestness they celebrated her mysteries.

As we have already stated, these Mysteries were
divided into two rites, or degrees, the less and the
great, the former being preparatory to the latter.
But though the less were in a sense preparatory to
the great, there is nothing to show that every
Mysta might become an Epopt, or, in other words,
that those learned in the lesser mysteries might, on
that account, claim initiation into the great. Initiation into the less was regarded as a religious act,
one that was in no wise to be omitted. Indeed,

initiation into these was thought by the Greeks to
be as necessary as baptism is among the Romanists,
and Terrence tells us that the custom of initiating
children was general.   But it was a more difficult
thing to gain admission to the greater.   The reason
for this may be inferred from what we have already
said.   The lesser had very little to do with doctrine, being for the most part *rites* and *shows*,
guarded by a thin veil of mystery, while the great
were to teach certain *doctrines* that, in the state of
the heathen world, the multitude were not prepared
to accept.[9]   The lesser taught, to be sure, the great
doctrines of an overruling Providence as well as of
a state of rewards and punishments, but it was for
the most part only a rehearsal of the story of Ceres
and Proserpine, accompanied with scenic representations; but the greater, the τελται, taught truths
which, had they become general, would have given
a mortal blow to the religion of the state.[10]   The
stories told of the institution of the lesser Mysteries, on the occasion of the visit of Hercules to
Athens, are fables.   It was doubtless in the plan
of the society to cause this division for the purpose
we have mentioned.   The hour when the most
sacred and holy truths could be openly proclaimed,

Warburton Div. Leg.   [10] Ouvaroff Eleus. Myst., 38.

had not then come to the world. The middle wall
of partition was as yet unbroken.

Eleusis, in which the Mysteries were celebrated,
is a little town of Attica, on the coast, north-west
from Athens. The rites were celebrated in the
magnificent temple built at the command of Ceres
herself. Such was the respect in which this temple
was held, that even Xerxes, the declared enemy of
the gods of Greece, and the destroyer of their temples, spared it. It was destroyed by Alaric, the
Balth, 396 A. D., in his wonderful march from
Asia Minor to Rome.

A description of the purifications and other ceremonies which filled up the first nine days of devotion, would be too tiresome to repeat. The Greeks
had built the particulars of these ceremonials upon
the wanderings of Ceres in search of her impris-
oned daughter. The ceremonies of the tenth day,
the day of initiation proper, are all we will describe.

On this day, a vast procession, each bearing the
narthex, a sort of hollow reed in which Prometheus
is fabled to have stolen the heavenly fire, left
Athens for Eleusis. It was a strange procession,
composed of the most incongruous elements, and
moving with a want of dignity that seems foreign
to the solemn scenes they were about to enter.

As the procession moved along, with here and there asses bearing the implements used in the rites,[11] laughter and gibes were heard on every side. Nearing the bridge that crossed the river Cephissus, a woman, or a man dressed as such, was stationed to represent Iambé, the servant who amused Ceres when sad from the loss of her daughter. This character was privileged to utter sarcasm the most biting, and taunts the most piercing, to those in the procession, more severe even than Aristophanes ever dared utter in his comedies.

Previous to his initiation, the candidate was closely questioned concerning his life, as it was required that he be of a clear and unblemished character, and free even from the suspicion of any notorious crime.[12]   He was even required to confess every wicked act he had committed during his whole life. Nor was a less degree of purity required of the initiated for their future conduct.   They were obliged by solemn engagements to commence a new life of strictest piety and virtue.   Indeed, among the ancients, initiation was regarded as a palingenesia (new birth) of corrupted human nature, the death of vice and the beginning of purity.

[11] Hence the proverb, "*Asinus portat mysteria.*"
[12] Libanius Decl. XIX.

There were four superior officers who assisted in the ceremony of initiation. These were the Hierophant ('Ιεροφάντης), the Torch-Bearer (Δαδοῦχος), the Sacred Herald ('Ιεροκήρυξ), and the Attendant at the Altar (ὁ ἐπὶ βωμῷ.) The Hierophant was regarded as the representative of the Creator, and bore as his symbol the Demiurgus, or golden globe. His surroundings were in keeping with his dignity, and wonderfully like a scene described in Revelation. His throne was golden, arched over with a rainbow, radiant with stars. Before him stood twenty-four attendants clad in white and wearing crowns of gold, while around him burned SEVEN lights, whose brilliancy was increased by thousands of burnished mirrors. His office was to instruct the neophyte, after he had passed the trying ordeal of initiation, in the true purport of the Mysteries, and to unfold the sublime truths which were there taught. The Torch-Bearer represented the sun, and the Attendant at the Altar the moon, and severally bore these symbols. Their office is sufficiently indicated by their names. The Herald was the representative of Mercury, the messenger of the gods, whom Jupiter sent to bring the stolen Proserpine to earth, and bore the caduceus, or wand, of Mercury, as his badge.

As the lustrations and initiations into the less Mysteries represented the wanderings of Ceres, and taught the minor ideas we have mentioned, of Providence and man's accountability, enforcing these with the authority of future rewards and punishments, it may not be uninteresting to show the manner in which this was accomplished. Led by the mystagogue, an office filled indifferently by those of either sex, the candidate approached the portal. The vicinity of the temple had previously been purged of all but the initiate, and all were forbidden to approach under pain of instant death. For the sake of greater security, the Herald proclaimed 'Εχὰς, ἐχάς ἐστε βέβηλοι, "Hence, hence, O ye profane," as the candidate was led into the sacred inclosure. It was for him a moment of extreme terror and solemnity. It was the time for him to call up all his firmness and fortitude. The poet Virgil, in his sixth book of the Æneid, which is supposed to be a description of the Eleusinian Mysteries, thus solemnly addresses the gods: "Ye gods, to whom the empire of ghosts belongs, and ye, O silent shades, and Chaos, and Phlegethon, places where silence reigns around in the realms of night, permit me to utter the secrets I have heard, give me your divine permission to disclose things buried in deep earth and darkness." Instantly all was confusion. The most horrible sounds assailed his terrified ears— the fierce roar of wild beasts, the hissing of serpents, the crash of thunder. Solicitude and total perplexity seized him. He was unable to move a step forward, or to find the entrance to that road which was to lead him to the place to which he aspires. Claudian, speaking of the entrance into these mystic rites, says, with a vividness that is poorly expressed in our language: " Now I see the shrines shake upon their tottering bases, and lightnings, announcing the deity's approach, shed a vivid glare around. Now a loud warring is heard from the depths of the earth, and the Cecropian temple re-echoes, and Eleusis raises her holy torches, the snakes of Triptolemius hiss and lift their scaly necks rubbed by their curved yokes. So afar the three-fold Hecate bursts forth."[13]

Passing on, the bandage was removed from his eyes, and he found himself in what appeared a wild, uncultivated country. A pale, spectral glare supplied the place of sunlight. Beasts of prey menaced him from every point, while the elements, unloosed, threatened him and the world with instant destruction. Recovering from his surprise and ter-

[13] De Raptu Proserpinæ.

ror, and his eyes being accustomed to the twilight
of the place, he discovers before him a door with this
inscription, "He who would attain to the highest and
most perfect state, and rise to the sphere of absolute
bliss, must be purified by fire, and air, and water."

Scarcely had he read these words, when the door
turned on its hinges, and he was thrust through
the entrance into a vast apartment. A loud plaint
of sorrow wailed through these shadowy corridors,
filling him with unutterable dread, while, at the
same time, two high iron gates crashed open, dis-
closing to his frightened view a vast, yawning gulf
of flame. All the pains and sufferings of grim and
dread Tartarus were made to pass before him. The
terrible purification of fire—the avenging furies and
forked tongues of flame; the purification of air—
the strong, burning wind and the mighty, rolling
wheel; the purification by water—the gloomy lake,
with its dense clouds and fearful shadows, all speaking of the most awful verities of religion, and declaring the great law of retribution, were some of
the sights that met his eyes.

In the sixth book of the Æneid Virgil gives
what is supposed to be a description of these
sights: "Before the very courts, and in the opening
jaws of hell, grief and tormenting care have fixed

their couches, and pale diseases; repining age, fear and famine—forms terrible to view—and death and toil, then sleep, that is akin to death, and criminal joys of the mind; and in the opposite threshold, murderous war, the iron bed-chambers of the furies, and frantic discord."

Hardly had these been passed, ere his way was barred by another iron door, before which he halted, while the Hierophant chanted, in a solemn voice, the Orphic poem quoted by Eusebius: "I will declare a secret to the initiated, but let the door be shut against the profane. But thou, O Musæus, the offspring of bright Selene, attend carefully to my song, for I shall deliver the truth without disguise. Suffer not, therefore, thy former prejudices to debar thee of that happy life which the knowledge of these sublime truths will procure unto thee, but carefully contemplate this divine oracle and preserve it in purity of mind and heart. Go on in the right way, and see the sole Governor of the world. He is one and of himself alone, and to that one all things owe their being. He operates through all, and was never seen by mortal eyes, but does himself see every one." This was the first intimation the candidate had of that sublime dogma, the Divine unity, which these Mysteries were about to unfold.

Scarcely were these words said, when the door
before which he was standing opened and disclosed
a scene of ravishing beauty, quite the contrast of
the scene of gloom they had left behind. "Here
the air they breathe is more free and enlarged, and
clothes the fields with radiant light. Here the
happy inhabitants know their own sun[14] and their
own stars."[15] These two so different scenes explain
what Aristides meant when he called the shows of
the Eleusinian Mysteries that most shocking and,
at the same time, most ravishing representation.

The initiated, who till now only bore the name
of Mystæ, are called Epoptæ, and this new vision
Autopsia. This Autopsia was the most sublime
part of the entire initiation. The candidate had
just seen the horrors of the lost, had looked into
the "very courts and opened jaws of hell." .Gloom,
darkness, and horror surrounded him ; when suddenly upon him burst the Autopsia, and listening
to his guide he is told, that in this light without
form was imaged the Divine splendor. In. this
beautiful sight of a light whose source was unseen,
but which illuminated all and spread its radiance
over all, was the symbol of the glory that dwelt

[14] It must be remembered that these initiations took place at mid
night.   [15] Æneid, Book VI.

visibly in the Godhead. It was a fore-gleam of that divinest truth of a one God, soon to be revealed, though imperfectly, for no Paul stood by with words of matchless power to declare to them this "unknown God." He was nevertheless made manifest, and in his unveiling the Epopta regained some of those precious truths that had been well-nigh lost in the shipwreck of humanity. "And now become perfect and initiated they are no longer under restraints, but crowned and triumphant they walk up and down the regions of the blessed, converse with pure and holy men, and celebrate the sacred Mysteries at pleasure."

Such is a hasty sketch of the scenes of the last day of the ten sacred to the Eleusinian Ceres, and it may not be uninteresting to know that where the temple stood at Eleusis, behind its site, on the western side, is still shown a terrace cut in the rock itself, some eight or nine feet above the floor of the temple. Its length is about two hundred and seventy feet, and its breadth in some places forty-four feet. At the northern end is to be seen the remnant of a chapel, leading up to which were several steps.

The question naturally arises, what truths were really taught, and in what manner? We have suf-

ficient authority for asserting that not only did the
Epoptæ acquire just notions concerning the Deity—
the relations between man and God—the primitive
dignity of human nature—its fall—the immortality
of the soul—the plan of redemption—and finally
another order of things after death, but that traditions were imparted to them, *oral*, and even *written*,
great thoughts saved, when humanity was wrecked.
We know as a fact that the Hierophant communicated to the Epoptæ certain sacred books, which
none but the initiated could read.   And it appears
from what Pausanias relates that some writings were
preserved between stones called *petroma* (Πέτρωμα),
which were never read except at night.[16]

In the closing scene of the celebration of these
mysteries, there is a curious phraseology used as a
benediction, Κόγξ, Ὄμ, Πάξ, *Conx, Om, Pax.* These
words were long regarded as inexplicable, but they
proved to be pure Sanscrit, and are used to this
day by the Brahmins at the conclusion of their
religious rites.[17]

The number of Epoptæ was always very limited,
even when the Mysteries had fallen into decline
(and they did decline most shamefully), but the
secret of the sanctuary was never violated.   For

[16] Ouvaroff, Eleus. Myst., 40, 41.   [17] Ouvaroff, 28.

four hundred years after the beginning of the Christian era they continued their initiations. Valentinian, who died in the year of Christ 374, would have destroyed them had it not been for the representation of his proconsul in Greece. In the general proscriptions of Theodosius the Great, they were included and destroyed.[18] Previous to this, however, a last and most desperate effort was made to purify them and restore them to their former influence, for this seems to have been the design of the Neoplatonists, such as Iamblichus, Porphyry, and Platinus. It was the vain death struggle of aged Polytheism with young Christianity, a struggle that could have but one end.

[18] A. D. 346–395.

Chapter III.

The Isianic Mysteries.

N entering upon our investigation concerning the Mysteries of Egypt, we are conscious that it is a subject of the deepest interest. Over the entire history of the Land of the Pyramids, a veil of mystery is drawn, thick as the fabled one that hid the face of Isis from the look of the vulgar. The very name calls up a host of strange scenes, and opens, like some magic "Sesame," the cavern door where lie hid untold riches of the days gone. Its history is a dream, not of the promises of the future, but of the achievements of the past. Here empire first placed her throne and swayed her scepter. Long before Greece, and Rome, and Assyria had been wrapped in their swaddling clothes, Egypt was a man of war, and the hero of victory. The stones that reared Athens in splendor, and spoke forth the beautiful conceptions of Phidias and Praxiteles, were unused in the quarries long after the Colossi of Thebes had grown old with years. While Abraham, the father of the faithful, wandered a nomad and lived in tents, a Pharaoh sat on the throne of Egypt, and but a few years after the Ishmaelitish merchants led their camels, laden with spices, balm, and myrrh, commodities only used by rich and cultivated peoples, from Gilead to the Nile. A few years from this, and there were standing armies in Egypt, chariots of war, bodies of infantry, and, what is still more surprising, a large body of cavalry.

Now it must be remembered that it was in the Secret Society of Isis and Osiris that this ancient and wonderful civilization had its origin. Here were fashioned and wrought out those ideas that subsequently entered into the very life of the people. It was undoubtedly its laws that gave Egypt such power. Its achievements can be read on the sculptured walls of Thebes and Memphis. Its ideas sit imperishably throned on the solemn stony faces of the Sphinx; and as these in their solitude look ever onward, it is the Isianic society incarnated, looking for the coming of the hour its priests and devotees longed and watched for, but which never came to them.

There is another reason why the history of this Society is of absorbing interest to us, and that is, the influence it had on the religion professed by so many millions, both on this continent and in Europe. There is no doubt but that the Jews were strongly inclined to the superstitions of the Egyptians. Their whole history in the wilderness shows this, and much of the ritualistic law given them was in compliance with this prejudice.[1] Those men who exercised a controlling and formative influence in the affairs of the Jews, were, without any question, initiates of this Society. Joseph, when exalted to the prime ministry of Egypt, was married by Pharaoh to the daughter of the priest of On, which is but another name for Heliopolis, or Thebes, the great seat of these Mysteries. By this marriage he became of the caste of priests, and eligible, both he and his descendants, not only to initiation, but to the highest offices in the rites. Moses, the son of Pharaoh's daughter, bred at court and instructed in all the wisdom of his day, must have been initiated in order to have learned this wisdom. But the most

[1] For a full discussion of this subject, vide Warburton's Div. Leg., Bk. IV, Secs. 2 and 6.

convincing proof of the influence of this Society upon the Jewish mind is found in that wonderful scene enacted at the base of the mount while the top was shuddering before the mighty presence of the great "I AM." The bull Apis was always, in Egyptian worship, the symbol of Osiris, and as they made the calf of gold and shouted, "These be thy gods, O Israel," they were copying precisely the worship of this Society in their adoration of Osiris, under his symbol.

But more to our purpose is the influence this Society had upon that of Pythagoras, in whose teachings we find the secret of the friendship of Damon and Pythias. This influence was not only suggestive, it was formative. In many cases we can trace the parentage of the ideas of the Samian to these Mysteries. Here he found that which he sought when he left his native isle intent upon penetrating the innermost secrets of things, not only of things physical, but things divine as well. His moral and religious ideas show their Egyptian origin. The unity of the Godhead, the immortality of the soul, and the necessity of an upright, virtuous life as the preliminary to happiness hereafter, which was inculcated in such a forcible way in the secret recesses of the Theban temple, all found a place in the Pythagorean society. His astronomical and geometrical ideas were derived from the Egyptian priests, and his mechanical ones also. The grandest achievements of engineering skill the world has ever seen are to be found on the banks of the Nile. Modern science stands aghast at the thought of rivaling them. It was while standing face to face with the problems solved in the erection of the Pyramids and Sphinxes, and in the transportation of the Colossi, that Pythagoras conceived that grandly beautiful theory of what may be termed in the language of a modern philosopher, "The rhythm of movement." We would not, however, be regarded as representing him as a servile copyist—far from this. But it is still true that the suggestion of many of his ideas may be traced to the teachings of the priests of Isis and Osiris.

The two central figures of these mysteries, as well as of Egyptian history, were Isis and Osiris. These, when stripped of their mystic garments and brought down to the level of humanity, appear to have been an early king (Osiris) and queen (Isis) of this country, who were at the same time brother and sister. These, by their superior virtue and intelligence, won the admiration and confidence of these wild and untutored barbarians, led them out of their degraded state, and guided their feet into the path of civilization and empire. Under their direction the land of savage darkness became light, and full of joy. Isis taught the people to hold the plow and turn the furrow, and to make bread from the ripened grain. While doing this she made laws for human society, and restrained men from lawlessness and violence by their sanction. Osiris built Thebes, with its hundred gates ; erected temples and altars, INSTITUTED THE SACRED RITES, and appointed priests to have the oversight and care of the holy things.[2]

Having accomplished these things, and seeing their effect upon his own people, he resolved to raise a great army, and, leaving Isis as ruler, go through all the world, "For he hoped he could civilize men and take them off from their rude and beast-like course of life."[3] This he succeeded in doing, but shortly after his return he was slain by his brother Typhon. After his death Isis made a vow never to marry again, and spent her days in ruling justly over her subjects—"excelling all other princes in her acts of grace and bounty toward her own people, and therefore, after her death, she was numbered among the gods, and as

---

[2] Diodorus Siculus, Bk. I, Chap. I.   [3] Idem.

such had divine honors and veneration, and was
buried at Memphis, where they show her sepulcher
at this day in the grove of Vulcan."[4]

This appears to be about the truth concerning
these mysterious personages, though the gratitude
of after ages invented an immense number of fabulous stories. The sacred rites which Osiris is said
to have instituted received many additions in course
of time, and finally were divided into two degrees.
These, as in their copy at Eleusis, were called the
Great and Less, the latter being a preparation to
the fuller revelation of the secrets contained in the
former.

In the Great Mystery was represented the allegorical history of Osiris, which the Egyptians regarded as the most solemn mystery of their religion,
and which Herodotus and all the other ancient
writers mention with the greatest caution. To be
initiated in these was the great privilege of the
priests, though this caste were not all admitted in-
discriminately to this honor. This was reserved for
the heir-apparent to the throne and for such priests
as excelled in virtue and wisdom.[5] This extreme
exclusiveness explains the conduct of the priests of
Thebes in delaying the initiation of Pythagoras, and

[4] Idem, page 28.   [5] Wilkinson's Ancient Egypt, Vol. I, 321

in yielding to his solicitation for this honor only at the positive command of King Amasis.

Such was the Great Mystery. The Less or initiatory degree had, however, no other purpose than the corresponding one at Eleusis ; namely, to teach the doctrine of an overruling Providence, enforcing it with the sanction of future rewards and punishments. The "work" of this degree was better adapted to the end in view than the Grecian copy. The famous myth of the "Judgment of Amenti," which forms a part of "The Book of the Dead," is without any question an account of this initiatory rite. To fully understand the scenes, we must remember that the candidate always represented one dead, and the entrance into the cavern in which the Mysteries were celebrated was allegorically the doorway to the grave.

Entering a vast chamber, the candidate found himself in the presence of Osiris, the dread and impartial judge of the dead. The way to this point had not been without its trials. At the entrance he had passed Cerberus, the hideous "devourer of the dead," ready with open jaws to do his terrible office, should he be found unworthy. Before Osiris were poised the scales of justice, near which stood Thoth or Time, and the dog-headed Anubis, "the

director of the weight." The candidate advanced
alone, in the attitude of prayer—a symbol that it
was on his own merits he was to be judged. Anubis placed a vase, holding a representation of the
heart of the applicant, in one scale, and the emblem
of Truth in the other. In silence all awaited the
result, while the dread Osiris sat with crook and
flail to pronounce judgment, and as the scale turned,
it was pronounced. If adverse, he was conveyed to
earth again, and as he passed out, all communication with the Mysteries was figuratively cut off, by
hewing away the earth with an ax, after his exit.
If, however, his virtues so far predominated as to
entitle him to admission to the mansion of the
blessed, Horus, taking in his hand the tablet of
Time, conducted him to Osiris, who sat on his
throne in the midst of the waters, from which rose
the lotus bearing upon its expanded flower the four
Genii of Amenti.

After passing the dread god, still guided by
Horus, disguised in the dog's head, the customary
mask of the attendants, the candidate threaded his
way through mysterious labyrinths, reaching at
length a stream of water, which he was directed to
pass. At the same time three grotesquely attired
forms stopped him and, pressing to his lips the

chalice of Oblivion, bade him "DRINK TO THE OB-
LIVION OF ALL VICES AND THE FORGETFULNESS OF
ALL IMPERFECTIONS."

The terrible scenes having been passed through,
the joy of the initiate began. Hymns, in honor of
the Divinity, were sung, choruses of triumph and joy
were heard. He listened to the most sublime doctrines of the sacred science. No more a profane, he
dwelt among the best and noblest of the land, among
the choice spirits of his beloved Egypt.

Such was the initiatory rite of Isis. It was the
idea here developed of a strict and impartial scrutiny of every man's life, one before which even kings
were found wanting, that gained for it such an influence over the Egyptian mind, and gave to the
civilization of the land of the Ptolemies its distinct
individuality and complexion.

The Great Mystery, as we have already hinted,
was founded upon the murder of Osiris and the
wanderings of Isis in search of his dismembered
body. The legend was this: On the return of Osiris from his journey of civilization, he fell a sacrifice to the intrigues of his brother Typhon, who
had formed a conspiracy to destroy him and usurp
his throne. Osiris was invited to a grand en-
tertainment, at which all the conspirators were

present. Typhon produced a valuable chest, or ark, richly inlaid with gold, and promised it as a gift to the one present whose body it would most conveniently contain. Osiris was tempted to enter it, but was no sooner in the chest than it was nailed down, and cast into the river.

The body thus committed to the waves was thrown up in Byblus and left at the foot of a tamarind-tree. Isis, in the extremity of her sorrow and bereavement, wandered over the earth in search of the body, and, after many extraordinary adventures, at length discovered and bore it back to Egypt in triumph, to give it a splendid interment. By the treachery of Typhon she was again deprived of the body, which was severed, and divided among the conspirators. With infinite zeal and labor Isis again discovered the remains, and committed them to the priests for burial, having first pledged them to secrecy, at the same time reporting that Osiris was risen from the dead.[6]

On this legend the dramatic scenes of initiation were constructed. They were pompous and imposing and conducted with great splendor. Several days were given up to them. In the procession were borne the images of Isis with the dog's head,

[6] Oliver's History of Init. Intro.

and the ark, or *cista*, emblematic of the one which held the remains of the murdered god. The procession was led by the priest or Hierophant of the mysteries, who bore in his hand a garland of roses. The statues of Isis were always crowned with wreaths of this flower, which gave rise to the phrase "*sub rosa.*" Those who desire a fuller account of these Mysteries will find it in Warburton's Divine Legation of Moses, Vol. II.

The places of initiation were contrived with much art and ingenuity, and the machinery with which they were fitted up was calculated to excite every passion and affection of the mind. These places were indifferently a pyramid, a pagoda, or a labyrinth, furnished with vaulted rooms, and extensive wings connected by open galleries, with huge pillars on which were carved the mysterious symbols used in the initiation. The island of Phile, in the Nile near the cataracts, contained a temple dedicated to Isis and Osiris, which covered nearly its entire surface. " It was in the gloomy and subterranean caverns of this temple that the grand and mysterious arcana of this goddess were unfolded to the adoring aspirant, while the solemn hymns of initiation resounded through the long extent of these stony recesses. It was there that Superstition, at midnight,

waved high her flaming torch before the image of
Isis, borne in procession, and there that her chosen
priests, in holy ecstasy, chanted their sweetest symphonies."[7]

These rites prevailed very extensively in the ancient world, especially in Greece.   In Rome, Isis
had several temples, the most important of which
stood in the Campus Martius.   In works of art, Isis
is represented as clad in a long tunic, and her upper
garment fastened on her breast by a knot; her head
is crowned with the rose and lotus.

The influence these Mysteries had on Egyptian
life was immense.   In these sacred retreats were
laid, and laid deep, the foundations of that civilization that is at the same time the wonder and problem of modern times.   Though the rites became, in
course of time, very much corrupted and licentious,
there can be no doubt of the fact that, in their early
existence, they did a great work for Egypt, and a
work that has more monuments still standing to
testify to its greatness, than any other of the many
Mysteries of the ancient world.

[7] Ind. Antiq., Vol. III, 536.

Chapter IV.

The Cabirian Mysteries.

N the northern part of the Ægean Sea, just off the coast of Thrace, lies a little island about thirty-two miles in circumference. From its center rises a lofty mountain called Saocé, from whose top the distant walls of Troy could be seen. Its political history was of little importance. It is said to have given birth to Dardanus, the founder of Troy. Its inhabitants fought on the side of Xerxes, at Salamis, and, in after years, it served as a city of refuge to the fleeing unfortunate.

But, notwithstanding the little account in which it was held politically, Greece always spoke of Samothrace with the greatest veneration. It called up to the Grecian mind things venerable from their antiquity, and to be reverenced by reason of their peculiar sanctity. The Mysteries which were here celebrated, next to those of Eleusis, were the most famous of the Hellenic world, and surpassed these and all others of Hellas in their antiquity. In the migration which the Egyptian gods made into the land of Hellen, they first celebrated their sacred rites on this island. So great was their antiquity, and so confessedly of Eastern origin, that the Cabiri never attempted to alter the language used in the celebration of the Mysteries, but, to their last day, made use of a peculiar dialect,[1] which was a compound of Hebrew and Chaldee. Iamblichus claims that the language used in these Mysteries was the "language of the gods, the first and most ancient language which was spoken on earth."[2] Indeed, such was the reverence in which the Cabiri were held, that those authors who mention them seem to shudder with superstitious dread at the very thought.

This very dread has closed the lips and held the stylus of those who could have given us information concerning these rites, and made the task of unfolding their secrets one of extreme difficulty. This remark applies as well to the other Mysteries, but not to such a degree as to the Cabiri. The knowl-

[1] Diodorus Siculus, Book V.   [2] Iamblichus de Myst., Sec. 7, chap. 4.

edge we have comes from putting together scattered hints of their nature and design, with the little aid we get from the questionable History of Sanchoniatho, preserved by Eusebius.[3] These fragments are full of apparent contradictions, and to this must be added the fact that their officiating priests were not infrequently confounded with the gods whom they worshiped, and both called by the common name, Cabiri. It is, indeed, difficult to keep this distinction in mind. Cabiri was the name of the gods worshiped, while the proper title of the priests was Coes.[4]

The Cabiri, according to Sanchoniatho, were the sons of Sydyk, but we are baffled at every turn, as we attempt to learn, except through conjecture, their birthplace and birth-hour. They were seven in number, were said to be skilled in medicine, and the builders of the first ship. This is all we know positively concerning these mysterious personages. The rites were probably introduced into the sacred isle by the Pelasgi,[5] the earliest inhabitants of Greece, and must have been celebrated for nearly two thousand years.

But, though our positive knowledge of the Cabiri

---

[3] Eusebius Præp. Evan., Lib. I, chap. 10.

[4] Κοίης ιερεύς Καβείρων, Heysch, 10.　　[5] Herodotus, Lib. II, 51.

and their Mysteries is so slight, there is a conjecture
that has so much circumstantial evidence to support
it, and at the same time such a great amount of
internal proof, that it may be regarded not in the
light of a theory so much as a determined fact.
This is the conjecture of Faber,[6] that these Mysteries were nothing more than an allegorical account
of the flood, and that the rites referred to the inci-
dents of the Deluge, and the Sabian worship of the
sun and stars, introduced by Nimrod.

His reasons for this conjecture are so curious that
we make no apology for introducing them here.
Taking the fact so frequently stated by ancient
writers, that the language of the Mysteries was of
Oriental origin, from the names of the deities he
shows conclusively that they are derived, for the
most part, directly from Hebrew words. And not
only so, but that the root words of these names had
some reference to the Deluge, or to the circumstances and persons connected with it. This resemblance is altogether too frequent to be simply
fortuitous. Thus, Titan, a word which occurs so
often, not only in these Mysteries, but in the whole
Grecian mythology, is evidently the Hebrew *Tit*
(טיט), and signifies a diluvian, or one living at the

[6] Faber on the Cabiri, Vol. I, 19.

time of the flood. *Sydyk*, the father of the Cabiri, is the same word Moses used in speaking of Noah, in Gen. vi, 9 (צדיק); while the very name Cabiri is only writing the Hebrew Cabirim (כבירים) in Greek characters. All these coincidents seem to point to the flood; but there is one other that is still more interesting—it is especially declared that the Cabiri were the builders of the first ship that was ever navigated.[7]

His conjecture as to the establishment of the Mysteries is also very plausible. After the wonderful preservation of the Cabiri in the ark, it would be very strange did not the descendants of Noah, and especially those who outrode the flood with him, commemorate this preservation by some special and solemn religious festival. This, in itself a thing most proper, soon lost its character of a simple festival, and became an act of worship—not to God, the Savior, but to Noah and his sons, the saved. These were elevated to the rank of Hero-gods. It was but a short time before this was still further corrupted by the introduction of Sabianism. The Chaldean shepherds, as they lay on the ground, in the still midnight, and gazed up into the blue above, and saw the stars holding their ways unchanged—Canopus

[7] Faber, Vol. I, chap. 1-3.

glittering down upon them with its diamond bright-
ness, Orion ever pursuing the wearied Pleiades, and
Lyra beaming down upon them so peacefully—felt
their souls awed within them; and, as there were no
singing angels to tell them a better story, they fell
down and worshiped. "Men began to build temples to the stars, to sacrifice to them, to worship
them, in the vain expectation that they should thus
please the Creator of all things."[8] For four hundred
years this idea, a remnant of the antediluvian idolatry, lay working in the bosom of the posterity of
Noah. Ham was especially tainted with it; but he,
as well as others, was prevented from openly avow-
ing it, through fear of the patriarch, who was still
living. At length Noah was gathered to his fathers,
and then a flood of Sabianism and idolatry, more
destructive than that above which the ark rode
safely, burst in. Nimrod, the first avowed apostate
after the flood, openly attempted to build a temple
to the host of heaven. Babel was God's answer to
his crime.

It was upon corrupted and mutilated traditions
of the Deluge that the Mysteries of the Cabiri were
founded. The union of Sabianism, or star worship,
with these traditions caused many peculiar ideas

[8] Maimonides.

and many apparent contradictions to creep into the
rites. While adoring the heavenly bodies, they
forgot not the object of the founding of the rites—to
commemorate the Deluge. Noah and the Sun soon
became one in their worship. The upturned cres-
cent of the waning moon, as it rode the heavens,
was no unfit emblem of the ark that rode the waters,
and they were soon worshiped in conjunction. The
Chaldeans became famous the world through for
their skill in astronomical science, and while they
marshaled the stars and called them by their names,
they contrived to picture upon the celestial sphere
the principal events connected with the Deluge.
Modern astronomy has continued the idea, and this
night Nimrod looks down upon the affairs of mortals from his shining place in Orion.

The scenes of the initiation, as we gather them
from the scattered hints that have come down to us,
seem to be an allegorical representation of the inci-
dents of the flood, beginning with the entrance into
the ark of those that had been chosen, and ending
with their exit into a new world and a new era.
That the candidate might fitly represent the up-
rightness and purity of the Noachidæ, he suffered
a preliminary purification by water and blood—a
strange likeness to the Jewish rites. As the past

was to be forgotten, all its instructions superseded and its foundations destroyed, even as the breaking up of the fountains made chaos of the antediluvian world, he was led to the fountain Lethe (oblivion) and made to drink forgetfulness, and then to another, Mnesmosyne (memory), that he might be prepared to remember the instructions he was about to receive.

Into the jaws of a mystic cavern, through ways covered with terror and gloom, thrust forward in the midst of most appalling sounds—the rushing waters, roaring thunders, expiring yells, flashing lightnings—the death-cries of a strangling, drowning world, his attendants, while about him and on either hand the spectral sins of his past life glared phantom-like upon him. To these succeeded silence and darkness, emblems of that which filled the ark as it wandered over the waste of waters seeking some friendly land on which to grate its keel. At length a feeble light diffused a spectral glare through the apartment in which the candidate rested. In its dimness and ghastliness, strange objects of terror met his sight. Black-draped walls, pictured with symbols of decay and death, were around him. Terrific phantoms grim and ghastly, passed and repassed, and at his feet up rose a bier on which was a coffin, and in the coffin a dead body. Invisible choirs chanted dirges, while other visions, more terrifying still, were multiplied around him, until, trembling and fearful, oftentimes senseless, the poor bewildered neophyte knew not which way to turn.

But here ended the pilgrimage of gloom. Suddenly a flood of dazzling light poured in upon the scene. The surroundings changed as if by enchantment. The dark drapery with its funeral emblems disappeared. Garlands wreathed the walls and crowned the altars. The dead in the coffin sprang to life, and the funeral psalm swelled into a joyful pæan of hope and victory. A new era had come to the world, and this was the emblem of its breaking. The candidate was led to the presiding priest and instructed in the secret science of the institution, which, in the main, was the same as that taught at Eleusis.

There was one part of the initiation that must not be omitted, as it throws much light on a certain passage in that most incomprehensible book, the Apocalypse. At the close of the "work" of initiation, the candidate was baptized and received, as in the Christian Church, a *new name*. This new

or baptismal name was engraved, together with a
mystic sign or token, upon a white stone, and served
as a talisman in time of danger, and as a sign of
recognition wherever he went.[9]   Strange stories are
told of its magic power.   It was an age of unkind-
ness, of any thing but union, and yet at sight of
this token, that mystical rather than magical communion of soul, called union, at once sprang into
being.   St. John must have referred to this *mystic
stone* when he wrote, " To him that overcometh,
will I give to eat of *hidden* manna, and will give
him a *white stone*, and in the stone a new name
written, which no man knoweth saving he that re-
ceiveth it."[10]

It is worthy of observation just here, that the
idea seems always to have prevailed among the initiated, that the groundwork of their Mysteries was
a sort of wonderful regeneration or new birth.   As
we have already stated, initiation was supposed to
be the beginning of a new life.   In its solemn and
terrific scenes, the old traditions and old life ended,
and out of it the candidate came with new thoughts
and new aims.   It was eminently proper, then, in
view of this belief, that a new name should also be
given him.   A strange and fearful scene took place,

[9] Arnold Rat. & Eth. of Free Masonry.   [10] Rev. ii. 17.

in these Mysteries, when this regeneration, by the
singular rites of the Taurobolium, was celebrated.
The high-priest, clad in his pontifical robes, de-
scended into a pit, above which was laid a floor,
pierced with innumerable holes.   Upon this floor a
bull, crowned with chaplets of flowers, was led, and
his throat cut.   The reeking blood fell in showers
upon the boards and, through the holes, upon the
priest below, covering his head, his body, and his
raiment.   This baptism of blood was conceived to
regenerate those upon whom it fell, and in token of
this new birth they wore their blood-stained garments as long as possible.   There is something
extremely strange and curious in this custom, especially to the believer in immortality and a resurrection.   This ceremony, doubtless, had reference to
the death and resurrection of the Hero-gods in whose
honor the Mysteries were celebrated.   It is a fact
full of meaning, that most of the ancient Mysteries
represented those who were their patrons as having
tasted death and afterward experiencing a miracu-
lous revivification.   Thus Osiris was dismembered
by his enemy, Bacchus by the Titans, Hercules,
Adonis, Mercury, Orpheus, were all dead and yet
lived again.   And it was in this strange and, in
some respects, horrible ceremony, that the candidate

was allegorically represented as undergoing the same events.

It should also be observed, in closing, that wherever the rites of the Cabiri prevailed, we always find them, in some manner or other, connected with caverns. The mysterious rites at Samothrace were performed in the cave Zerinthus or Saon. About the entrance were clustered immense swarms of bees, emblematic of that new birth which was to be found in its recesses. Within the cavern stood a huge pyramid, inclosing in its massive sides the central chamber, in which the most sacred rites were performed. So, also, the Taautic cross (T), either simple or compound, and a small lake with a floating island, were found. The use and meaning of all these will be sufficiently manifest to those who have followed us in our account of this peculiar rite.

That strange and mysterious third sect of the Jews, the Essenes, that existed in Judea in the time of Christ, owes its origin probably to suggestions received from this society, through the Tyrian architects, at the time of Hiram. No one can read the account Josephus gives of this sect without being at once struck with the similarity in form to the Cabirian rites. But though, in symbol and rites, it corresponded, its ideal was infinitely more exalted and beautiful—so exalted that there is a strange likeness between it and that of Christianity. This likeness is so great that De Quincy does not hesitate to express his conviction that the Society of the Essenes was nothing but another name for Christianity, and that the early Christians were forced to take this form to protect themselves.[11]

[11] Historical and Critical Essays, page 39, et seq.

Chapter V.

Pythagoras.

THE authentic facts in the history of Pythagoras are so few, and the sources from
which they are gathered of such a comparatively recent date and so untrustworthy, that it
is impossible to give more than a bare outline of
his personal history. This is to be regretted, as,
after all, the true history of an age is condensed in
its biographies. In the ceaseless tide of matter,
ships are destroyed, cities overturned, and fields
devastated, but this is a very small part of history.
There are other reasons why cities are burned than
burning torches, and these reasons are to be found
in the personal histories of the men of an age. It
is in proportion as we understand the man, and only
so, that we understand the elements in which he

worked.   When we have made of the dead a friend, and brought him to life again, and let him teach us to see with his eyes and feel with his heart, to love the things he loves and mingle with the friends among whom he moves, we shall know more of his generation and circumstances than all mere history books can teach us.

The influence Pythagoras had, not only upon his own age, but upon all others, makes us regret our ignorance the more.   In his own age, without friends or wealth, by the mere power of intellect, he wrought a regeneration among a people, that has rarely, if ever, been equaled in human history.   And on after ages his influence has been immense.   Plato, whom Emerson calls " the balanced soul," and whose works, " The Bible of the learned for twenty-two hundred years," is greatly a debtor of Pythagoras.   His philosophy bears, on nearly every page, the imprint of the Samian.   His wonderful Phædo, one of the grandest books mortal ever wrote, is probably only a statement of the Pythagorean doctrine of immortality, which he learned from Simmias and Cebes. And his Timæus is also Pythagorean in its sentiment.

There are several circumstances that conspire to render the task of the biographer of Pythagoras a

difficult one.   The absence of any written memorials
coming from Pythagoras himself, and the scantiness
of the notices of his contemporaries—being, for the
most part, merely incidental—make the attempt to
write his life full of labor.   But more baffling than
these is the secrecy thrown around the constitutions
and actions of the Pythagorean brotherhood.   With
a fuller knowledge of these, we could at least con-
struct a mental history of the philosopher; but we
are met, in our attempts to do so, by the inventions
for which this very secrecy furnish such an opportunity.   The fables thus imagined and told were
easily caught up by the Neoplatonic writers, to
whom we are indebted for most of our information,
and with whom nothing was too strange or incredi-
ble if it related to a god, or what was divine.   To
understand how easily such stories were made, and
how readily they were believed, we need only refer
to the scores of absurd and whimsical tales that are
told as solemn facts concerning the history and
methods of initiation of the various Secret Societies
of to-day.   These tales, often senseless and self-
contradictory, are accepted by sensible people as
veritable history, and told with a gravity that is
laughable, and an earnestness worthy of a better
cause.   Diogenes Laertius thus mentions some of

these fables concerning Pythagoras.[1] "He is said
to have been a man of the most dignified appear-
,ance, and his disciples adopted an opinion concerning him, that he was Apollo, who had come from
the Hyperboreans ; and it is said that when he was
stripped naked, he was seen to have a golden thigh.
And there were many people who affirmed that
when he was crossing the river Nessus, it addressed
him by his name."

It is to this work of Diogenes Laertius and that
of Iamblichus, that we are mainly indebted for whatever we know of Pythagoras, the work of Aristotle
concerning the Pythagoreans being unfortunately
lost. In the use of these, as well as the works of
Porphyrius and Philolaus, our own judgment must
tell us what to receive and what to reject.

That Pythagoras was the son of Mnesarchus, who
was either a merchant or a seal engraver, may be
safely affirmed.[2] He was born at Samos, (an island
off the coast of Asia Minor, south-west from Ephe-
sus,) and was connected by race with the Tyrrhenian Pelasgians. These latter were the descendants
of the Pelasgi, the earliest inhabitants of Greece, the
founders of the Cabirian Mysteries, and had scattered themselves over various parts of the Ægean

[1] Diog. Laert. Lives of Phil. Pyth. IX.   [2] Herodotus IV, 95.

Sea. The facts for fixing the date of his birth are for the most part few and indistinct. The best authorities place it at 608 B. C., others still later. All agree, however, that he flourished at the time of the reigns of the brilliant but wicked Tarquinius Superbus at Rome and Polycrates at Samos. Cyrus, of Persia, had also at this time led his shepherd warriors down from the mountains, and had established the Persian empire at Babylon.

The conditions of his birth and his education rendered him eminently fitted for the task before him, namely, the establishment of a brotherhood the purest the world has known, and, if we are to judge of it by the friendship of Damon and Pythias, the best it will ever know.

As we have already stated, he was by birth a Samian, and by descent a Tyrrhenian Pelasgian, and the conjecture of Ritter,[3] that through this descent, as by birthright, he became the possessor of a certain secret and peculiar cultus, is doubtless true. It was his great ancestor, Pelasgus, who established the famous Cabirian Mysteries, the prolific mother of so many others. These, in common with the other Mysteries, partook of a religious character. They were jealously guarded from the

[3] Ritter Gesch. Pyth. Phil.

intrusion of the foreigner, and were handed down from generation to generation as a sacred heritage. As a Pelasgian, it can not be doubted that he became possessor of its secret, and it is not improbable that, in the midst of the solemn and impressive scenes of his initiation, he first conceived the idea of his society. It is asserted that at his first initiation he was so impressed with the idea, that something more than the priests were able or willing to explain was intended to be conveyed by this solemnity, that he resolved to devote his life to the discovery.

His education was of a nature to develop this idea. After receiving instruction from Thales, the father of Greek philosophy, and others of the early Greek philosophers, who were astonished at his quickness of understanding, he traveled into other lands. It was the current belief of antiquity that Pythagoras had undertaken extensive travels, and had visited not only Egypt, but Arabia, Phenicia, Judea, Babylon, and even India, for the purpose of collecting all their scientific knowledge, as well as learning their ideas of God. For the furtherance of these objects, he was initiated into the sacred Mysteries of each of these nations. In another part of this work[4] we have taken occasion to speak

[4] Chapter I.

of the mighty influence these mysteries have had on civilization and the progress of mankind.

Suffice it to say here, that these Mysteries were not only the repositories of the deepest and most sacred religious truths, but they were more—they were the source of all ancient moral life, the schools of philosophy, science, and literature. They went ever in the van of progress, and taught to the select few the truths the world was not ready to receive. In these were wrought and fashioned those social and moral ideas that afterward passed into the every-day life of the peoples of these ancient empires. It was impossible, then, that Pythagoras could properly work out his system without being initiated in these.

Provided with a letter from Polycrates, the Samian king, to Amasis, king of Egypt, he journeyed to that country, to which every Greek had learned to look with a great curiosity. Here, after a tedious probation, he was initiated into the Mysteries of Isis,[5] passed the dreaded Osiris, drank oblivion of vice, and was found worthy to hear the words of wisdom that for so many ages raised Egypt so far above the other nations in civilization. From the land of the pyramids he went to India, to learn

[5] Ritter Gesch. der. Pyth. Phil.

the wisdom of the Gymnosophists, visiting the Chaldeans and Magi on his way.[6] In Judea, Babylon, Phenicia, and other places, he sought wisdom, worked out his ideal society, and, at the age of forty, returned to his native Samos with a mind deeply impressed with his divine mission.

Nothing certain is known concerning the length of time spent by Pythagoras in Egypt and the East, nor the duration of his residence at Samos, nor the influence his principles had obtained previous to his removal to Italy. Ritter, basing his belief upon certain remarks of Herodotus, is inclined to think that the mysteries of Pythagoras had obtained some footing in Samos, and that he had attracted many disciples to himself before he chose Croton as the center from which to radiate his ideas. He certainly had obtained a great influence and inspired his age with reverence previous to this removal.

In his visits to the various places in Greece—Delos, Sparta, Crete, Phlius—he appears in a priestly or religious character, or as a lawgiver. During a visit to Phlius, King Leon, its ruler, asked him concerning his profession. He modestly replied he "was a philosopher"—lover of wisdom—asserting that the name sage or wise belonged only to divinity.

[6] Diog. Laert. Life of Pyth., Book VIII, iii.

The reason of his removal from Samos to Croton, in Italy, is doubtful. It is highly probable that the condition of his native country, while under the rule of the unprincipled Polycrates, was not at all favorable to the realization of his schemes. His idea embraced politics—the science of government as well as religion and philosophy—and he doubtless wished to put these ideas into a practical form, as he afterward did in Magna Græcia. The tyrant who had put one of his brothers to death, and banished the other, that he might be sole ruler, would be little likely to tolerate a system which was oligarchal, if not republican, in its essence. So, though his admirers were content to believe that the good opinion of his fellow-citizens so overburdened him with public duties that he had no time for the study of philosophy, and so withdrew from Samos, it is not at all probable when we remember the character of Polycrates. In this belief we are strengthened by a letter from Anaximenes to Pythagoras, preserved in Diogenes Laertius.[7]

ANAXIMENES TO PYTHAGORAS.

"You are more prudent than we, in that you have migrated from Samos to Croton, and live there in

[7] Life Anaximenes, Book II, iv.

peace. For the descendants of Æacus commit un-
heard-of crimes, and tyrants never cease to oppress
the Milesians. . . . . But you are beloved
by the people of Croton, and by all the rest of the
Italians, and pupils flock to you even from Sicily."

But though this explains the reason of his withdrawal from Samos, it gives us no clew to his choice
of Croton as a residence. Grote, in his history of
Greece, thinks it may have been the celebrity of
this city for the cultivation of the art of medicine,
that had some influence on him.

But whatever the reason may have been, the result proved the wisdom of his choice. Previous to
his arrival at Croton, the inhabitants of Magna
Græcia had been notorious for the looseness of
their manners. They were licentious and vicious
to the last degree. On one hand no attention was
paid to those moral principles which constitute
moral government, and on the other to those civil
ones that form the basis of all civil rule. Marvelous stories are told of the effect of his eloquence
upon the people of Croton, of the magic power of
his words as he exhorted them to abandon their
luxurious and corrupting manner of life, and devote
themselves to that purer system he came to introduce. Under his influence, Sobriety, Temperance,

Justice, and Virtue soon took their proper places.
Justice and equity appeared in the administration
of the laws, and as a result, a high degree of prosperity was reached.   His adherents were chiefly of
the noble and wealthy class.   Three hundred of
these were formed into a select club, or society,
bound to each other, and to Pythagoras, by solemn
vows, for the purpose of living the life of asceticism
he marked out, and studying his religious and philosophical theories.   His doctrines spread rapidly
over Magna Græcia, and clubs of a similar character
were established at Sybaris, Metapontum, Tarentum, and other cities.   Of the peculiar nature of this
society, both as to its external and internal arrangements, we shall have to speak in another chapter.
It is sufficient for us here to follow the history of
Pythagoras and his society.   This three hundred
of Croton speedily gained an extensive political influence.   That this influence should be wholly on
the side of aristocracy, or oligarchy, (though Diogenes asserts it was republican,) resulted naturally,
both from the nature of the Pythagorean society
and from the constitution of the three hundred.
As the general of a powerful and well-disciplined
order, Pythagoras, of course, exercised considerable
influence, both in the affairs of Croton and the other

cities of Magna Græcia.   It does not appear, however, that he ever held any official rank, though the
Senate urged him to accept the office of Prytanus,
or President, of the oligarchy.

It is easy to understand how this aristocratical
and exclusive club would excite the jealousy and
hostility of the democratic party in Croton.   The
support which it lent the oligarchal party in the
various cities, the secrecy of its proceedings, and
the exclusiveness of its spirit, produced against the
whole system a wide-spread feeling of hatred.   This
hatred speedily led to its destruction.   In the hos-
tilities which broke out between Sybaris and Croton,
brought on by a refusal of the latter (to which they
were urged by Pythagoras) to surrender some fugi-
tives of Sybaris,[8] the forces of Croton were headed
by the Pythagorean Milo, and the other members
of the three hundred doubtless held prominent
places.   The decisive victory gained by the Crotoniates seems to have elated the Pythagorean brotherhood beyond measure.   A proposal for a more democratic form of government, arising from a refusal
on the part of the Senate, to distribute the newly
conquered lands among the people, was unsuccessfully resisted by the Pythagoreans.   Their enemies,

[8] See Chapter VII.

headed by Cylo, who had unsuccessfully sought initiation into the Society, excited the populace against them. An attack was made upon the house of Milo while the three hundred were gathered there. The building was fired, and many perished, only the younger and more active escaping. Similar commotions arose in the other cities of Magna Græcia in which Pythagorean clubs had been formed. These were at last quieted through the influence of the Peloponnesian Achæaus, but as an active and organized brotherhood, it was everywhere suppressed, and did not again revive, though it was a long time before it was put down in the Italian cities. Still the Pythagoreans continued to exist as a sect, the members of which kept up among themselves the religious and scientific pursuits peculiar to themselves.

As to the fate of Pythagoras, there is considerable uncertainty. One account makes him perish in the house of Milo, with his associates. Another tells that he fled to Tarentum, and being driven thence, he escaped to Metapontum, and there starved himself to death. His tomb was shown at Metapontum as late as the time of Cicero.

Some accounts imply that Pythagoras had a wife and grown daughter when he went to Croton, while others state that he married Theano, a lady of that city, and had two children.

His general bearing, which is of so great importance to one who aspires to be a leader of men, was very striking. In his youth, his personal appearance was so handsome as to have obtained for him the surname of the Samian Comet, or the fairhaired Samian. From his well-known influence, it is certain that in his maturity he was no less a type of manly beauty. From the pictures drawn of him by Porphyry, Laertius, and Cicero, there appears to have been something very dignified and almost superhuman in his appearance. He wore a white robe and moved with a dignity and grace that inspired all with reverence. Remembering this, we can not wonder at his successful advent at Croton, nor at the divine honors paid him after his death.

We have but little evidence as to the amount or kind of knowledge that Pythagoras acquired. Without any direct testimony, however, it might be safely affirmed that his attainments were of no mean nature. The very remarkable influence he exerted, not only over his immediate followers, but over those in other cities—the tinge his views gave to after philosophy, (witness that of Plato, for example,) and even the many marvelous stories told of him, prove him to have been a man of singular abilities and wonderful acquirements. Indeed, we have the direct testimony of several writers that he was a man of extensive learning. The great prominence given in his system to geometry is evidence that the statement with regard to his mathematical researches is well founded. He is said to have discovered the proposition that a triangle inscribed in a circle is right-angled, and also the celebrated forty-seventh problem of Euclid, that the square of the hypothenuse of a right-angled triangle is equal to the sum of the squares of the other two sides.

Discoveries in astronomy are also ascribed to Pythagoras. There can be little doubt that he paid great attention to arithmetic, and its application to weights and measures, and the theory of music. He is also mentioned as being a proficient in medicine.

The religious element was predominant in his character, and it was doubtless a religious asceticism, in connection with a certain mystic religious system, that he endeavored to secrete. It was this religious element that made the profoundest impression upon his contemporaries. So deep was their reverence that they regarded him as having a peculiarly close connection with the gods. The Crotoniates even identified him with the Hyperborean Apollo, and he himself shared the same views, regarding himself as gifted with divination and prophecy and as the revealer of a purer and holier mode of life.

As to the morals of Pythagoras, they were certainly in advance of his time. In an age of gluttony, drunkenness, and most notorious licentiousness, he taught the severest abstinence, and a life of most exemplary purity. Drunkenness he called an expression identical with ruin. It is said of him that "he was never known to have eaten too much, or to have drank too much. He abstained wholly from laughter and from all such indulgence as jests and idle stories, and when he was angry he never chastised any one, whether slave or freedman."[9]

His maxims and rules all show his superiority to the spirit of the age. He forbade men to pray for any thing in particular because they do not know what is good for them. He also forbade the offering of victims to the gods, commanding his followers to worship only at those altars that were unstained with blood. His principle with regard to oaths has a wonderful similarity to the New Testament precept, "Swear not at all." Cultivated trees, and animals that do not injure men, were not to be destroyed or

[9] Diog. Laert.

injured. Nothing should ever be said or done in anger, and gratitude to the gods should be shown by the singing of hymns.

It has been a matter of dispute, whether Pythagoras left behind him any writings. Many works have been ascribed to him, and several lists have been made of them, but it is extremely doubtful whether any genuine works of his are extant. It is probable, from the pains which he took to confine his doctrines to his own school during his life, that he never committed his philosophical system to writing. The celebrated golden verses attributed to him, are ascribed to some of his followers. They may be taken, however, as a brief summary of his doctrines.

Such was the man who founded the school in which Damon and Pythias were taught; a man pure in an age of impurity, just when injustice reigned, abstemious when self-indulgence was the rule, and, above all, *true* in the midst of deceit and falsehoods.

Chapter VI.

The Pythagorean Society.

TO understand the secret of the wonderful friendship of Damon and Pythias, we must know something of the nature of that Society whose teachings produced this as a result.

In itself, it is worthy of the closest study. It embodies the germ of the philosophy of that king among philosophers, Plato. Some of its speculations are grand beyond expression. It deals with the most sublime things of time and space, in a spirit and with a depth of insight that was unsurpassed in that age, and knew no equal, until he of the Academy spoke.

But this is only a part, and a very small one, of its claims upon our consideration. It is the effect it had upon men that chiefly makes it worthy of our attention ; it is because there was something in it that made men kinder and better, and more helpful each to the other, something that made the hearts of its members aglow with gentle and generous affections, that made them respond to the thrill of mercy and glow with nobleness, that it becomes of value to us to know what it was.

Damon and Pythias are not its only exemplars to the world. Archytas, saving the life of his friend Plato at the court of the younger Dionysius, as Pythias did that of Damon at the court of the elder, and Simmias, willing to share the odium and even to suffer the penalty of the escape of his master Socrates, are other examples of the power this Society had to produce that rarest of all virtues, friendship.

The age of the world in which this Society flourished must not be forgotten. It was not in the nineteenth century, after eighteen hundred years had taught men lessons of helpfulness and made the great idea of the brotherhood of man, through the fatherhood of God, something beside a juggle of words, but it was in an age whose vocabulary knew no such word as humanity, whose utmost ideas were bounded by self—an age that was unkind and cruel, just emerging from the twilight of barbarism into the light of civilization. Out of such an age came the Pythagorean Society, and out of this Society—Damon and Pythias.

In inquiring into the nature of the Pythagorean Society there are three points that claim our attention : First, its composition ; second, its observances ; third, its principles.

In a previous chapter,[1] we have spoken of the club of three hundred which was formed at Croton on the arrival of Pythagoras, and which eventually became the ruling body of that city. It must not be inferred, however, that this was the number of adherents in this populous city. The Society was by no means as select as this. These, undoubtedly, lived in a closer and more intimate fellowship with Pythagoras, and were admitted to secrets and had revealed to them deeper principles of his system than the multitude, yet his society must have been vastly greater than this three hundred. This was the nucleus of his society. It is contrary to the nature of man to believe that this number of men, avowedly having a certain secret as a bond of union, could have ruled in a city as large as Croton without sharing that secret, at least partially, with their followers. Indeed, it is quite well ascertained

[1] Chap. V, page 80.

8

that it was hatred against the Society, on the part of a Crotoniate, who was refused admission to it, that led to the overthrow of the government.

We also know that several women were among the adherents of Pythagoras, and also that none of these were members of this select company. The adherents were divided into two general classes, termed estoric (ἐσωτερικοί) and exoteric (ἐξωτερικοί). These terms were not so much the names of degrees as they were terms used to express the advancement the initiate had made. At the expiration of his novitiate, and upon his initiation to the first degree, he was exoteric, and was called Acousmatici.[2] The second step was to become Mathematici. Upon the third advancement he ceased to be exoteric, and became esoteric, and was in the highest sense a Pythagorean. These were permitted to see the master, and hear from his lips the more remote and subtle principles of his philosophy.

In regard to the observances and discipline of the Fraternity, there is the same lack of positive information that we have already regretted in other connections. It was an old Pythagorean maxim that every thing was not to be told to every body, and they certainly lived up to this precept. All ac-

[2] Iamblichus, chap. 17.

counts agree that whatever was done and taught among the members was kept a profound secret from all without. Even among the members themselves there were different degrees in the confidence bestowed—a distinction arising not from any thing external, but from merit alone. The novitiate required of the candidate before he was admitted to the Mysteries, was long and severe. This severity did not consist, as has often been affirmed, in bodily torture, tearing the flesh with heated pincers, or cutting it with sharp instruments, but was rather a trial of the candidate's power of maintaining silence.[3] A silence of five years was imposed upon the candidate, but was sometimes lessened in the case of one who manifested an aptitude for the Pythagorean doctrine. This trial was intended to abstract his mind from material things, and enable him to reflect with undivided attention on the ineffable nature of the Deity, and thus to arrive at true wisdom. Even after this trial, the candidate was rejected if found passionate or intemperate, contentious, or ambitious of worldly honors or distinctions. Only he who passed these severe trials was allowed to enter into the arcana and know the symbolism of these things. Whoever was not willing to endure them might with-

[3] "A still tongue marks a wise head."

draw without opposition, and a tomb was erected to his memory, as if he were dead.

That there were certain observances of an ascetic nature, something like those of the Romish monasteries, in the life which the members of the brotherhood led, is pretty certain. By some, Pythagoras, following the Orphic precept, is represented as forbidding all animal food. If this was the case—and that it was, generally, is very probable—it must have arisen from his belief in the transmigration of souls, or the metempsychosis. That the man who forbade the beating of a dog, asserting that he recognized in its voice the soul of a friend, should for some like reason forbid the killing or eating of animals, is not at all strange. It is probable, however, that this prohibition could not have been universal. Some of the members, Milo, the athlete and general, for example, could not possibly have dispensed entirely with animal food. According to one authority, only the flesh of oxen used for plowing, and that of rams, was forbidden. Similar uncertainty exists in regard to his prohibition of fish and beans.

But whatever special articles may have been forbidden, temperance of all kinds seems to have been enjoined, and the entire training tended to produce great self-possession and mastery over the passions.

The principal meal consisted of bread, honey, and water, and it is asserted that they had a common meal, resembling the Spartan syssitia, at which they met in companies or messes of ten. Each contributed regularly a certain share to the common stock, and at these messes no distinction was known.

For a description of the daily routine of the members, we are indebted to Iamblichus. This suggests many points of comparison with the ordinary life of a Spartan citizen. They rose before the sun for religious worship; verses from Homer were recited, music was introduced to rouse their mental powers. Several hours were then spent in severe study, followed by a pause for recreation. Indeed, it is not unlikely that many of the regulations of Pythagoras were suggested by what he saw in Crete and Sparta.

Among the best-ascertained features of the Pythagorean brotherhood, is their devoted attachment to each other. It was a maxim of Pythagoras that the two most excellent things for man were to speak the truth, and to render benefits to each other. In a wonderful degree the thought of this maxim became wrought into the very life of his followers. It was no dull, cold, formal thought to them, but a living, controlling principle. It is this

chiefly that makes the study of his system valuable.
Were it only from its determining connection with
Damon and Pythias, a knowledge of it could not be
useless. That which has formed such matchless
characters, that which has made men forget for a
time the selfish "Me," and live, and die if need be,
for another, can not but be something noble.

This friendship was all the more noticeable, as
we have already said, because it was at war with the
spirit of the age. All feeling was local—all was
Spartan, or Athenian, or Corinthian—not Grecian.
Many attempts had been made to unite the different
States of Greece, but though they were in part successful, the bond was, at best, very weak, and liable
to be broken on the slightest provocation. To build
in the midst of so much individualism a society
that produced, as its legitimate result, Damon and
Pythias, was a wonderful deed, and the methods
employed demand the closest attention of every ob-
server. Especially should each one who calls himself a Knight of Pythias study it well, that he may
emulate the character of his great patron.

There has been much questioning as to whether
Pythagoras had any distinct political design in
founding his brotherhood. That his institutions
were not intended to take those who adopted them

from the active pursuits of life nor from political duties, is certain. He aimed rather to produce a calm bearing and elevated tone of character, which those trained by the discipline of Pythagorean life should exhibit in their personal and social capacities, reflecting in these that order and harmony which exists in the universe. But notwithstanding the political power to which the three hundred arrived, it is very questionable if this entered into the original design of the founder. One of the best authorities says: "We can not construe the system of Pythagoras as going further than the formation of a private select order of brethren, embracing his religious fancies, ethical tone, and germs of scientific ideas, and manifesting adhesion by those observances which Herodotus and Plato call Pythagorean orgies and mode of life. And his private order became politically powerful because he was skillful or fortunate enough to enlist a sufficient number of wealthy Crotoniates, possessing individual influence, which they strengthened immensely by thus regimenting themselves in intimate union."[4]

When we come to inquire what were the philosophical or religious opinions held by Pythagoras, we are met at the outset, by the difficulty, that

[4] Grote's History Greece, Vol. IV.

even the authors to whom we must refer possessed no authentic records bearing date of the age of Pythagoras. If he, or any of his immediate followers, wrote any thing, it perished with them, or soon after. The probability is, he wrote nothing. The statements to the contrary prove worthless on examination. Every thing bearing his name is spurious. It is reasonable to suppose this from what little knowledge we have of the nature of his society, and especially from the profound secrecy observed in regard to his mysteries, not only toward outsiders, but even among members of the brotherhood. It is not at all likely that Pythagoras would expose to the chance of being learned in an hour those secrets for which, before imparting, he demanded a long novitiate. Nor would he throw open to the vulgar those ineffable holy things that could only be spoken of by those of a pure life.

It is almost certain that Philolaus[5] was the first who published the Pythagorean doctrine in a written form. Still, there is so marked a peculiarity evidenced in the Pythagorean Philosophy, by whomsoever written, and so many points of resemblance may be traced in the system, by whomsoever developed, that there can be no doubt but that we

[5] See infra.

have the germs of the philosophy of Pythagoras, as derived from its founder himself. There seems to have been the same earnest endeavor to preserve its original form as exists among the various Secret Societies of to-day to preserve their traditions and work uncorrupted. We hear of members being expelled for introducing innovations, and there was, even in antiquity, a sharply drawn distinction between genuine and spurious Pythagorism. Though doubtless, in the course of time, after it had passed through various developments, and through the hands of adherents of various tendencies, varieties made their appearance ; still, in the time of Philolaus, (about B. C. 430,) but a little more than one hundred years after the death of Pythagoras, we can safely affirm that no great changes had been allowed to creep in.

With Pythagoras, as with every other religious teacher, the first question presented for solution was concerning the origin of the Universe. It is by no chance that inspiration pens as its first words, " In the beginning." It is the great problem that presses for an answer every hour of one's life, and men will not follow any religious teacher who will not stand as a mouth-piece between them and the earth, and endeavor to translate the mystery of its origin.

Pythagoras attempted to solve, by a single principle this vast problem. Like his master, Anaximander, he abandoned the physical solution of the earliest Greek philosophers and passed from the province of Physics to Metaphysics, founding the third school of Greek Philosophy. The older of these philosophers regarded water, air, or fire, as the original principle. Those of the later Ionic and the Eleatic were pantheistic, but Pythagoras found the origin of all things in numbers, and as the solution given to this great problem is in all systems the fundamental idea, number was to the Pythagorean the all in all, not only the origin, but the "dominant and self-produced bond of the eternal continuance of things."[6]

Aristotle says: "Since of all things numbers are by nature first, in number, they (the Pythagoreans) thought they perceived many analogies to things that exist and are produced, more than in fire, and earth, and water; as that a certain affection of numbers was justice; a certain other affection, soul and intellect; another, opportunity. And, moreover, seeing the affections and ratios of what pertains to harmony to consist in numbers, they supposed the elements of numbers to be the elements of all

[6] Philolaus.

things."[7] Number, then, was the starting-point of the Pythagorean Philosophy. In numbers and their relation to each other, they found, or conceived they found the absolutely certain principles of knowledge. Nay, they even thought that numbers were things themselves, not merely representatives, but realities.

Number they divided into three forms, the even and odd, and a third resulting from a union of the other two, called the even-odd. This latter was an even number composed of two uneven ones.

The odd numbers he regarded as limited and perfect; the even, as unlimited and imperfect. This idea of the limited and unlimited played an important rôle in this system. It was the union of these two opposites that produced all being. One of the first declarations of Pythagoras was, that all things in the universe proceed from a combination of the limited and unlimited.

The analogies Pythagoras conceived to exist between numbers and geometrical figures, and especially the attributes of mind, is not the least curious part of his philosophy. In these relations, angles were especially prominent. Thus, according to Philolaus, the angle of a triangle was consecrate

[7] Aristotle Metaph. I, 5.   Also, XIII, 3.

to Kronos, Hades, Pan, and Dionysius; the angle of
a square to Rhea, Demeter, and Hestia ; the angle
of a dodecagon to Zeus.   The perfect square represented the Divine mind.   The cube was the symbol of the mind of man after a well-spent life, equal
in all its parts, and fitted for a life with the celestial
gods.   One was a point, two a line, three a surface,
four a solid, five represented quality and color, six
life, seven intelligence and health, eight love, friendship, understanding, insight.   Marriage, justice, and
other like things, were connected with various numbers.   Though not a number, while speaking of this
symbolism it may not be amiss to speak of the sig-
nification of the letter Y, which represented the
course of human life.   Youth arriving at manhood,
sees two ways before him and deliberates which he
shall follow.   If he meet with a guide who directs
him to pursue philosophy, and he procure initiation,
his life shall be honorable and his death happy.
But if he omit to do this and take the left-hand path,
which appears broader and better, it will lead to
sloth and luxury, will waste his estate, impair his
health, and bring on an old age of infamy and
misery.[8]

Musical principles also played an important part

[8] Stanley Lives of Philos.

in this system. The ideas of odd and even Pythagoras regarded as impossible of union had not
harmony stepped in. This harmony was regarded
as the regulating principle of the whole universe,
not only as an art to be judged of by the ear, but
as a grand principle running through all nature and
all mind, bringing order out of disorder, being out
of chaos, uniting into one glorious whole elements
that by nature were antagonistic. His idea of the
creation of all things was simply that by the union
of the limited and unlimited in accordance with
harmony, all things were produced. Just the manner of this is not so clearly seen. Indeed, just here
was the weak point of the Pythagorean philosophy.

There was an application of this theory of harmony that has passed into language and given to it
one of its most beautiful figures. The intervals between the heavenly bodies were supposed to be
determined by the laws and relations of musical
harmony. Hence arose the celebrated doctrine of
the harmony of the spheres, for the heavenly bodies
in their motions could but give rise to a certain
sound depending on their distances and velocities,
and as these two elements were determined by the
laws of harmonical intervals, the notes altogether
formed a grand harmony, a hymn of the spheres.

There is sublimity in this thought that we of this prosaic age do not realize. We, of to-day, talk learnedly of the nebular hypothesis, and mumble over the formula "inversely as the square of the distances," and think we have gone to the root of the matter. Perhaps we have, but were we to unstop our ears the sublime conception of Pythagoras might be realized to us now, though in a higher and better sense. This harmony, as he taught, is not heard, either because we have been accustomed to it from the first, and have had no opportunity of contrasting it with silence, or because the sound is so powerful as to exceed our capacity of hearing.

Fire had also no inconsiderable a place in the Pythagorean cosmogony. It was regarded as occupying the most honorable position in the universe, both at the center and in the remotest region. Philolaus calls this central fire the hearth of the universe; the house or watch-tower of Zeus; the mother of the gods; the altar, and bond, and measure of nature. Not only was it thus honorable in position, but in office it was equally noble, being the life-giving principle of the universe; though by fire in this connection is doubtless meant something more ethereal than the common element, fire.

Round this central fire the heavenly bodies performed their circling dance (χορεύειν), on the outer
verge the fixed stars, then in their order the fire
planets, the sun, the moon, the earth, and a curious
body, the counter-earth (ἀντίχθων), a sort of other
half of the earth introduced probably to make up
the number ten, since the *decade* was the perfection
of numerical harmony. This idea of a revolution
around the central fire included the idea of a revolution of the earth on its axis, thousands of years
before Galileo said, "It moves."

Perfection was thought to depend upon the dis-
tance from this central fire. Thus, the inhabitants
of the moon were more perfect and beautiful than
those of the earth.

Virtue followed the same law. It belonged to
earth only in an imperfect form. Wisdom in its
perfection, also, was enjoyed only in the *kosmos*—
the region beyond the moon.

Life was an attribute of all things, and was divided into four grades, united in man, the life of
mere seminal production, which is common to all
things, vegetable life, animal life, and intellect or
reason. The universe was regarded as having life
in itself, not as being produced or created, but,
only developed. Philolaus says the universe "is

imperishable and unwearied ; it subsists forever, from eternity did it exist, and to eternity does it last, one, controlled by one akin to it, the mightiest and the highest."

The Deity was spoken of as one, eternal, abiding, unmoved, like himself, alone—pervading the whole universe, though distinct from it, and was called the absolute *good*. The origin of evil was to be found not in Deity, but in matter which prevented the Deity from working out his purposes and conducting every thing to the best end. They also believed in an all-pervading soul of the universe, distinct from this Deity, probably being only the ever-working energy of the Deity. It was from this Deity that the soul of man proceeded, it being regarded as a number or harmony. So far as the soul was the principle of life in man, it partook of the nature of the central fire. It was divided into two elements, a rational, which had its seat in the brain, and an irrational one, which comprised the passions, and lived in the heart. The latter was believed to perish, but the former was immortal, because it had an immortal origin. Even animals had a germ of reason. Only their defective organization and the want of language prevented its development. The transmigration of souls was regarded only in the light of a purification. Souls under the dominion of sensuality either passed into the bodies of animals, or, if incurable, were thrust down to Tartarus, to meet with expiation or condign punishment. The pure were exalted to higher modes of life, and finally to an existence without a body.

Happiness consisted in the perfection of the virtue of the soul ; hence their maxims related more to the restraint of the passions, especially anger, and the cultivation of endurance, than to science.

Likeness to Deity was to be the object of all endeavors, man becoming better as he approaches the gods, who are the guardian and eyes of men, guiding the reason as well as exercising an influence over external circumstances. Man's soul was a possession of the gods, confined at present in the body, as a species of prison from which he had no right to free it by suicide.[9] With this idea of Divine influence was attached that of the influence of dæmons and heroes. (Socrates dæmon.) Music was regarded as having great influence over the passions. Self-examination was strongly insisted upon. In a word, it was a system, that for that age of the world was wonderfully pure in its *prac-*

[9] Phædo.

tice, and as to its fruits, wherever we hear of them, we usually hear of its producing men of great up-- rightness, conscientiousness, and self-restraint.

Chapter VII.

Croton, Sybaris, Syracuse, and Dionysius the Elder.

ANY account of Pythagoras, no less than of Damon and Pythias and their times, would be incomplete without some allusion to the Greek colonies in which they lived, and where they acted.

The names Greece and Grecian, or, as they were termed in the times of Damon and Pythias, Hellas and Hellenes, did not indicate a country marked by any geographical lines, nor a people dwelling in what we now know as Greece, but included the whole body of Grecians, in whatever part of the world they might be settled. Thus the inhabitants of Trapezus, on the farthest shores of the Black Sea, and of Massalia, in the south of Gaul, and of Cyrene, in Africa, were as essentially Grecians as the inhabitants of

Athens and Sparta. They all gloried in the name of Hellenes, boasting of their descent from Helen, and frequently asserted their right—one only those of pure Grecian blood could claim—of contending in the Olympic games and other national festivals of Greece.

Croton was especially noted for the number of prizes its inhabitants had gained in Olympic games.

It would be foreign to our purpose to enter into any extended account of these colonies, and we purpose merely a brief narration of the history of those connected with the story of Damon and Pythias, and of Pythagoras and his society.

We do this, in part, to show that Damon and Pythias were, in every sense of the word, Grecians. The common history of that wonderful people was theirs. Its literature and traditions were their birthright. The tales of valor and daring, the stories of adventure, the divine and heroic characters which Homer and Hesiod sung, were all theirs, by right. As Greeks, though distant from the fair skies of Attica, or the rugged hill-sides of Sparta, they worshiped the same deities as were adored in Hellas; and the sacred fire which was kept constantly burning on the public hearth was taken from the Prytaneum of the city from which the colony swarmed.

As a general rule, these colonies were more democratic in their ideas than the mother cities. This is but following a general law of all new settlements. Ancient customs and usages can not be preserved as at home. Men are thrown more into the society of each other. Those who, in older communities, surrounded themselves with a certain unapproachableness, can not maintain this in a new land. Common hardships shared, common difficulties overcome, and common dangers faced, place men more on an equality. Hence we find it difficult for a man, or a class of men, to exercise a permanent authority over other colonists. This explains the love of freedom so prevalent in these cities of Magna Græcia, and which Damon manifested in so eminent a manner, in opposing the designs of Dionysius. Owing to the freedom of their institutions, and their favorable position for commercial enterprises, many of the Greek colonies became the most flourishing cities in the Hellenic world.

The colonies of Sicily, of which Syracuse was the principal, began to be founded soon after the first Olympiad, 776 B. C. The greater part of Sicily was at this time inhabited by rude tribes, who were easily driven, by the Greeks, into the interior. The fertility of the soil, combined with the ease of acqui-

sition, soon attracted numerous colonists from various parts of Greece, and the coast of Sicily was
rapidly surrounded by a chain of most flourishing
cities.   Of these, Syracuse became the most powerful.   It was founded by the Corinthian, Archias,
734 B. C.   At the height of its power, it numbered
500,000 inhabitants, and was surrounded by a wall
twenty-two miles in circumference.

The history of this city is veiled in obscurity until the fifth century B. C.   During this century two
desperate attempts were made to capture it—one by
the Carthaginians, under Hamilcar, the father of
Hannibal, and the other by the Athenians.   The
first attempt was made 480 B. C., on the very day
that the Greeks gained the brilliant victory over
the Persians at Salamis.   Gelon, with 50,000 foot
and 5,000 horse of the Syracusians, after a bloody
and desperate engagement, defeated Hamilcar with
an army of 300,000, destroying 150,000, and captur-
ing the greater part of the remainder.

The other attempt, as having a direct bearing
upon our subject, demands a more extended notice.

It was in this attempt to capture Syracuse, that
the Athenian power, which had become so strong in
Greece as to overshadow all the other States, was
broken.   Some time about the year 428 B. C., the

feuds of race, which had been so disastrous to the rest
of Greece, broke out in Sicily. The Dorian cities
of the island, with Syracuse at their head, joined the
Peloponnesian Confederacy, and declared war against
the other cities. These latter applied to Athens for
help, and an expedition was sent against Syracuse,
but proved a failure, and its leaders were either fined
or banished. In the year 415 B. C., Athens, con-
ceited in her own strength, and urged to the under-
taking by the ambition of Alcibiades, decided,
contrary to the advice of her best citizens—Socrates among the number—to attempt the conquest
of Sicily.

The departure of the armament was a spectacle,
imposing in the extreme. At day-break the chosen
body of troops marched from Athens to Piræus to
embark, accompanied by nearly the whole population. One hundred war vessels, each with three
banks of oars, received them. As the ships were
preparing to slip their moorings, the sound of the
trumpet enjoined silence, and the voice of the herald,
accompanied by the people, was lifted up in prayer.
But one of that vast force returned to tell of its
fate.

This force, augmented to more than eight hundred vessels, after some delays reached Syracuse,

and began its investment. At first they were successful, the Syracusians even sending messages to Nicias, the Athenian commander, to treat of terms. Overconfidence on the Athenian side, and the arrival of aid from the Spartans for Syracuse, combined perhaps with treachery on the part of Nicias, changed the fortune of war.

To understand the plan of the battle which decided the fate of Syracuse, it will be necessary to give a description of the city. It consisted of two parts, the inner and outer city, as they were termed. The former of these—the older settlement—covered the rocky islet of Ortygia, the latter covered the high ground of the peninsula north of Ortygia, and was completely separated from the inner city. This island, to which the modern city is confined, is of oblong shape, about two miles in circumference, and is admirably situated for defense, lying across the narrow entrance to the port of Syracuse, with the Great Harbor on the west and the Little Harbor on the east. The island is separated from the main land by a narrow channel, which had been bridged over by Gelon. The Great Harbor is a splendid bay, about five miles in circumference, while the Little Port was spacious enough to receive a large fleet of ships of war. The city was surrounded by

a wall, and was also defended by the nature of
the ground. West and north-west of the outer
city stood two unfortified suburbs called Tyché
and Neapolis. It was doubtless at one of these
places that the villa of Damon was situated, and
whither he hastened at the time of his six-hour
reprieve.

In this Great Harbor the decisive battle was
fought. The Syracusians had blocked its entrance
with a line of ships moored across it, and as the
Athenians were already, according to the custom
of those days, beached inside, they were cut off
from all hope unless they could succeed in forcing
this line, and thus escape. Their fleet still numbered one hundred and ten triremes, or three-decked
vessels, which were furnished with grappling-irons,
and a large body of land forces to act as marines.
Previous to entering into the fight, Nicias, their
commander, addressed them in a stirring speech,
setting before them the fact that not only their own
fate but that of Athens depended on the events of
that day.

Dr. Smith, in his History of Greece, has given
a graphic description of this event, which we copy
entire.

"Never perhaps was a battle fought under cir-

cumstances of such intense interest, or witnessed
by so many spectators vitally concerned in the result. The basin of the Great Harbor, about five
miles in circumference, in which nearly two hundred
ships, each with a crew of more than two hundred
men, were about to engage, was lined with spectators ; while the walls of Ortygia overhanging the
water were crowded with old men, women, and children, anxious to behold a conflict which was to
decide the fate of their enemies, if not their own.
The surface of the water swarmed with Syracusian
small craft, many of them manned by youthful vol-
unteers of the best families, ready to direct their
services wherever they might be wanted.   The
whole scene, except in its terrible reality, and the
momentous interests depending on it, resembled on
a large scale the naumachiæ exhibited by the Roman emperors for the amusement of their subjects.
The Syracusian fleet, consisting of seventy-six triremes, was the first to leave the shore. A considerable portion was detached to guard the barrier
at the mouth of the harbor.   Hither was directed
the first and most impetuous attack of the Athenians, who sought to break through the narrow opening which had been left for the passage of merchant
vessels.   The onset was repulsed, and the battle

then became general. The shouts of the comba-
tants, and the crash of the iron heads of the vessels
as they were driven together, resounded over the
water, and were answered on shore by the cheers
or wailings of the spectators, as their friends were
victorious or vanquished. For a long time the
battle was maintained with heroic courage and
dubious result. At length, as the Athenian vessels
began to yield and make back toward the shore, a
universal shriek of horror and despair arose from
the Athenian army, while shouts of joy and victory
were raised from the pursuing vessels, and were
echoed back from the Syracusians on land."[1]

The Athenians succeeded in saving only sixty
ships (about half of their fleet), while the Syracusians were reduced to fifty.

Demosthenes and Nicias urged the Athenians to
make one more attempt, but in vain. The forty
thousand troops on land started for the interior,
closely pursued by the victorious Syracusians. At
the end of the sixth day's march but ten thousand
were left, and these surrendered at discretion.

Syracuse at the time of this struggle with Athens
was ruled by an aristocracy, with Hermocrates at
its head After the repulse and utter destruction

---

[1] Smith's Student's Greece, pp. 342-3.

of the Athenian armament he was for a time the idol of the city, but his life is only a repetition of that of every other ruler of Syracuse at that time. About 410 B. C., the democratic party coming into power, he was banished, and Diocles, the leader of the popular party, became undis- puted master of the Syracusian government. This Diocles was the author of the famous code of laws which bears his name. These, though demo- cratic in their essence, were of such a just and equitable character, that they continued in force long after Syracuse had fallen under the dominion of the tyrants, and indeed as long as the inhabit- ants were allowed to be governed by laws of their own.

But republics are proverbially ungrateful, and the history of Diocles forms no exception. Two years after his accession to power, being unsuccessful in battle, he was in turn banished. Upon this, Her- mocrates made a last desperate attempt to re-enter the city and regain the power, but was slain in the attempt, 407 B. C., and the city still remained a republic.

In this attempt of Hermocrates, the most brilliant ruler Syracuse ever had, and the one most inti- mately connected with our history, came into notice.

This was the celebrated Dionysius the Elder, who was born 430 B. C., and was, consequently, but twenty-three years of age at this time. He was the son of Hermocrates, another of the same name as the banished, and at this time dead, ruler of Syracuse. Dionysius was of humble origin, but had received a good education, and began life as a clerk. He had taken an active part in this unsuccessful attempt of Hermocrates, and was so severely wounded as to be left for dead, a circumstance which saved him from the sentence of banishment pronounced upon the adherents of Hermocrates. Left in the city, such were his address and talents that he soon placed himself at the head of the aristocratical party, and also gained influence with the people so rapidly, that on the deposition of the Syracusians, who had been unsuccessful against the Carthaginians, he procured his appointment as one of their successors. It was but a short time before his colleagues were dismissed on charges of treachery and corruption, instigated by Dionysius, and the latter was appointed sole general with unlimited and irresponsible power.

This position by no means implied the exercise of sovereign power—Syracuse was still a republic, and the Ecclesia, or assembly of the citizens, still met. But every measure of Dionysius showed but too plainly what was his aim, and we may date from this period the beginning of his tyranny or reign, which lasted without intermission for thirty-eight years. Asserting that an attempt had been made upon his life, he procured a body-guard, which a too subservient Senate speedily increased to one thousand. At the same time he induced the Syracusians to double the pay of his troops, and remove officers not favorable to himself and replace them by creatures of his own. In a little time he found himself strong enough to procure the condemnation of the leaders of the opposite party, and with these banished, an army officered by his creatures, and a servile Senate, at the early age of twenty-five, he openly *seized* the supreme power, B. C. 405.

His first operations in war were unsuccessful, and his enemies, embracing the opportunity, stirred Syracuse to revolt, and proclaimed a republic. For a moment they were successful, and the followers of Diocles were again masters of the city, but the sudden return of Dionysius from his camp at Gela disconcerted their plans and compelled them to flee from the city.

The power of Dionysius was now absolute, and he gave his whole attention to strengthening it both at home and abroad. The island Ortygia was converted into a strong fortress, and only his immediate attendants were allowed to dwell upon it. Another revolt broke out, but was soon crushed, and from this time his rule was undisputed, he having greater power than any other Grecian ever enjoyed, with the possible exception of Alexander the Great. By the year 384 B. C. he had possessed himself of the greater part of Sicily, and a considerable portion of Magna Græcia, and had raised Syracuse to be one of the chief Grecian States, second in influence, if indeed second, to Sparta alone. Under his sway, Syracuse was strengthened and embellished with new fortifications, docks, arsenals, and other public buildings, and became superior even to Athens in extent and population.

Dionysius died 367 B. C. Love of power was his ruling passion; the desire of literary fame, the second. In his manner of life he was moderate and temperate; but he was a stranger to pity, and never suffered it to check him in the pursuit of his ends. Though courageous, he was so fearful of treachery, as to live a life of constant dread, suspicious even of his nearest friends and relatives. The story of Dionysius and his flatterer, Damocles, well illustrates his uneasiness.

The character of Dionysius was not all that has been represented. Many of the stories related of him are doubtless gross exaggerations. But though this is true, the hatred of his character was not altogether undeserved. He was undoubtedly a man of great energy and activity, but he was altogether unscrupulous, and had no thought beyond his personal aggrandizement.

Such a man was it who was so moved at the unwavering friendship of Damon and Pythias, and in view of his character and suspicious nature, we can wonder but little that it was so surprisingly strange to him. It was a new revelation—a manifestation of human nature to him in a new light—a revelation little short of divine; but recognizing its nobility, the king became the suppliant, and the captive the benefactor.

A few words concerning Croton and Sybaris will close our account of the Greek colonies. These two cities, which hold such an important place in the history of Pythagoras and his society, were the earliest as well as the most prosperous of the Greek settlements in Southern Italy, or Magna Græcia, as this territory was called. They were both situated on the Gulf of Tarentum, both settled from Achaia, and their lands were conterminous. Cro-

ton was situated not far to the west of the south-
eastern extremity of the gulf. On this promontory
was built the magnificent temple of Here, or Juno.
A solitary column of this temple is the only remnant of the grandeur of Croton. Sybaris was further
up the gulf, where it makes its deepest indentation
in the land. An idea of their situation may be
easily got if we remember that the general shape
of Italy is that of a foot, with the toes to the west-
ward. Croton is on the heel of this huge foot,
while Sybaris is near the ankle. Of these two
cities, Sybaris was the oldest, having been planted
in the year 720 B. C. It had not much the advantage of its rival and neighbor, however, as Croton
was founded only ten years after, or 710 B. C.

The fatal conflict between these two cities, fatal
not only to Sybaris, which was razed to the ground,
but to Croton and the other cities of Magna Græcia,
took place 510 B. C., after they had enjoyed two
hundred and ten years of uninterrupted prosperity.
In this time, the position these cities had attained,
not only in material splendor, but in the intellect-
ual world, was surprising. It did not, to be sure,
equal the prosperity of the settlements in our own
country during the same number of years, but it
was astonishing nevertheless. We do not know,

however, the particulars of their increase. The
general facts of their size, wealth, and power, are
all that have come down to us, but these sufficiently
attest their magnificence. The walls of Sybaris
were six miles in circumference, while those ·of
Croton were twice as large. Both had powerful
allies, both were the mother cities of other colonies,
and their dominion extended across the Calabrian
peninsula, from sea to sea. Their great wealth is
shown by the fact that five thousand horsemen,
clothed in magnificent attire, formed a part in the
procession in certain festivals of the city, while
Athens, in her best days, could boast no more than
twelve hundred.

The fatal battle of Tracis was fought, as we have
said, 510 B. C. In the circumstances which led to
the struggle, there is no doubt but Sybaris was the
aggressor. Owing to internal dissensions in this
city, some five hundred of the wealthiest citizens,
who were members of the oligarchal party, had been
banished, and their property confiscated. They fled
to Croton, and in accordance with the custom of
the times, threw themselves as suppliants on the
altars for protection. A body of powerful exiles,
harbored in a city only twenty miles distant, naturally excited alarm at Sybaris, and its ruler, Telys,

demanded their surrender, threatening war in case of refusal. Croton was in consternation. Its neighbor, Sybaris, was decidedly superior, but on the other hand, it had always been regarded as an act of impiety toward the gods, and one they would visit with swift and sure punishment, to surrender a suppliant. The fear of the Crotoniates was on the point of overcoming their respect for the rights of asylum, but at length the persuasion of Pythagoras determined them to risk any hazard rather than incur the dishonor of betraying suppliants.

On their refusal to surrender the exiles, the Sybarites, three hundred thousand strong, marched to enforce their demand. At the utmost, one hundred thousand men were all the Crotoniates could muster, but with these, under the command of Milo the Pythagorean, and most celebrated athlete of his time, they advanced to meet the enemy. A bloody battle was fought near the river Tracis, in which the Sybarites were utterly routed with prodigious slaughter, while the victors, fiercely provoked and giving no quarter, followed so hot in the pursuit that they took the city, dispersed its inhabitants, and crushed its power in the short space of seventy days. So eager were the Crotoniates to render the site of the city untenable, that they turned the course of the river Crathis, so that its bed lay through the heart of the city.

The destruction of Sybaris excited the strongest sympathy throughout the Hellenic world, and was productive of the most serious consequences. From its fall may be dated the decline of the Grecian power in Magna Græcia. One strong power that held the natives of Italy in check was destroyed, and the other cities found it more and more difficult to repress the Osco-Pelasgian tribes. The Eternal City had already begun its course of empire, and this in the North, and Syracuse in the South, soon proved too strong for the weakened colonies of central Italy.

Chapter VIII.

Damon and Pythias.

THE story of Damon and Pythias, is one that "the world will not willingly let die." For nearly half man's historic life has it stood forth with a beauty and luster that an advancing civilization and a higher idea of humanity's claim upon humanity has in no wise dimmed. Other deeds and other men have come to be forgotten or despised. Year after year is making the world better, purer, holier. The kingly ideas that sway men's hearts are less savage every hour. The thoughts that were the guiding ones of last year, this finds too narrow, if not positively base. Some murderous Barabbas may be welcomed with shouts to-day, but it is the rejected and despised Christ that lordly centuries call Master.

But in the midst of these changes, the story of
the friendship of Damon and Pythias has in no degree lost its power over men. No nobler instance
of self-sacrifice, no more sacred example of true
friendship, relieves the long dark story of selfishness
the world has been writing with its blood. The
Christian of to-day, no less than the heathen of that
olden time, is moved to admiration and stimulated
to emulation by its recital. It is a story that belongs to no age or clime, but to humanity, forever
and always.

And there is reason that this should be so. The
men who, in the long run, have governed the world,
have been those who knew the human heart, those
who caught the sound of its beating and marched,
in their life journey, to its time and tune. Such
men are truly kings, not by any priestly anointing,
but in the only true sense, "*Dei gratia.*" These,
though they have never worn the purple, nor chilled
nations with fear, have a kingdom without metes
and bounds, with a reign whose duration knows no
"*Le roi est mort.*"

In this view Damon and Pythias are of the royal
house of humanity. Crowns were their birthright,
and empire their heritage—an empire, not over acres
and houses, but over lives. Life is every year reck-

oned more internal. Not slaughtered millions, not boundless wealth, measure life, but the inner acts of man, the kindness that prompts to deeds of mercy, the benevolence that takes form in charity, and, above all, the spirit of true love resident in man, that has sent him forth into the world, a messenger of good tidings, God's almoner of peace. These are the things that make up life.

Here is the secret of the influence this friendship has had. It is because it realizes the ideal of true life, because it is in accordance with the spirit of the perfect age of which every man's heart has a prophecy, and which causes him to recognize a kin in whatever is like it.

For a confirmation of our words, we ask the reader to go no further than the history of the Order of the Knights of Pythias. Its founders, deeply moved themselves by the simple touching story, thought they saw in it the lesson that would teach men their holiest duties, and join heart to heart in firmest bonds of friendship. They told the story, and besought men to join with them in proclaiming its evangel. One after another heard the message gladly, and, bowing about the altar, pledged hand and heart, even unto death. To-night, as the evening shadows fall, and the sound of the gavel clinks out into the darkened air, 100,000 of God's freemen will answer, and own they are bound to be faithful and true, even till their hearts are frozen into silence.

Of the personal history of Damon and Pythias, we know very little. When they were born, how they lived, or when they died, no one in their day took the trouble to note down. They stand forth from their own age, known only by one act; but they stand brilliant as a form of light in the darkest midnight. It might gratify our curiosity to know more about the details of their lives, to have answered those two questions that always force themselves upon us — Whence? whither? And yet perhaps it is better as it is. If we would know what manner of men they were, and what manner of life they lived—I mean true life, not eatings and drinkings—all that we need is to enter into the spirit of the act that has made their name to endure as long as there is a true brave heart to admire true bravery. When we have done this, we shall know their lives better than any chronology of events could teach us.

These two friends, Damon and Pythias, lived in Syracuse at the close of the fifth and beginning of the fourth century B. C. At this time Syracuse was in the zenith of its power. Hasdrubal and the

Carthaginians, and even Athens with its powerful armaments, were forced to own this island city as victor. It swayed an empire such as no other Greek city ever ruled. This prosperity was due to the superior talents and administrative abilities of the elder Dionysius, who had seized the government of the city, and overturned the democracy previously existing there. It was at the time of this usurpation of Dionysius that the events occurred that have made the names of these two Syracusans historic. They were both followers of Pythagoras, members of his society, which continued to exist years after the destruction of its political power, and appear to have been thoroughly imbued with the ideas of this wonderful man. The teachings they received within the secret recess of this Fraternity seem to have given a decidedly democratic basis to their minds. Not that republicanism was distinctly taught in the Pythagorean system, but the whole tendency of its precepts and, above all, the fraternity that it insisted should exist between its members, could but foster and develop a strong ·democratic feeling. So we find that while one, Pythias, was a soldier by profession, and had taken an active part in the wars which his native city was constantly waging with the Carthaginians, and the other, Damon, had given himself up to philosophical pursuits, they had equally an ardent patriotism and a determined hatred of tyranny. The constant wars in which Syracuse was engaged, and the internal strife consequent upon the changes of rulers, made it comparatively easy for a successful general, were he ambitious, to possess himself of the rule of the city. Hence, changes of government were frequent and violent. Aristocracies were supplanted by turbulent democracies, and these gave way, in turn, to despotic rule. These latter were called tyrannies by the Greeks, a name, as is well known, referring rather to the mode in which power was gained, than to that in which it was exercised.

It was such a series of events that led Damon to the act, that, but for the ardent friendship of Pythias, had cost him his life. As we have narrated in another place,[1] at the time of the Athenian invasion 413 B. C., the government was in the hands of a mild aristocracy, with Hermocrates as its leader. On his banishment, three years later, a democracy, with Diocles at its head, took its place. Under the new *régime*, Damon and Pythias both occupied prominent places, Pythias in the army and Damon in the Senate. The fate of Diocles is uncertain.

[1] Chapter VII.

He is reported to have slain himself for a violation of one of his own laws, which forbade any one, under pain of death, to enter the Senate Chamber armed. After the death of Diocles, the government remained still a democracy, but Dionysius now began plotting its overthrow, slowly at first, as he was not sure of the army. Damon, suspecting the designs of Dionysius, watched him closely, and overhearing an officer tampering with the fidelity of some troops, interfered in such a manner that his life nearly paid the forfeit, being saved only by the timely aid of Pythias and his great popularity among the soldiers.

Fearing that this was but the precursor to still more violent measures, Damon hastened to the Senate Chamber, while his friend sought the house of his expectant bride. Arriving at the Senate his worst fears were confirmed by the presence of a large body of soldiery, a thing positively forbidden by law. His astonishment was still further increased by a proposition to allow Dionysius a large body-guard. Nothing daunted by the outcries and tokens of dissent of the senators, Damon raised his voice against this violation of law, and at last despairing of his country's liberties were the tyrant permitted to live, attempted to take his life. It was an act worthy of the best days of Roman patriotism.

Foiled in his attempt, Damon was hurried away to instant execution, while Dionysius, artfully taking advantage of the situation, succeeded in having the guard doubled. In the mean time, Pythias, knowing in part the designs of the tyrant, and fearing his great patriotism would lead his friend into danger, hastened from the side of his bride to the Senate House in time to see Damon hurried to execution, he having been denied a few hours' respite to bid his wife and child good-by. Pythias earnestly joined his supplications to those of Damon, offering to take his place and be surety, even to death, for the return of his friend. The tyrant, struck by this strange offer, and fearing, perhaps, the influence of Pythias over the soldiery did he refuse, consented to the exchange, allowing the captive six hours to go and return, assuring him if he were not back by sunset his friend Pythias should suffer in his stead. Damon hastened from the city to his villa in the suburbs, while Pythias, in chains, was thrust into a dungeon.

Dionysius, as we have stated in a previous chapter, was by nature very suspicious, having no faith in the pretended friendships of those about him, and even denying that there was any such thing. On such a man, the willingness with which Pythias took Damon's place, could but make a deep impression. Still incredulous, he disguised himself, and going to the prison, endeavored to persuade Pythias to flee, offering him every inducement and bringing every argument to bear, to shake his determination.

While Dionysius was striving thus, the bride of Pythias, whom he had left unwedded at the altar that he might rescue his friend, came into the prison, and falling before him, besought him, by all the inducements she could bring, to fly, and pointed to the vessel with sails unfurled, that had been prepared to convey him to another land. It was a terrible trial to which Pythias was subjected. The tyrant's positive statement that Damon would not return, the safety promised by the awaiting ship, and, above all, the beseeching bride giving open expression to her doubts of Damon's faithfulness, and begging in agony that she might not see Pythias die on her expected wedding day, formed inducements almost too strong for human nature to resist. But resist he did, and back to the dungeon he went to await the dread hour.

While affairs were thus in Syracuse, Damon,

mounted on a swift horse and attended by his faithful freedman, had sped to his home, and without telling his family the reason of his haste, said farewell, and was about to return to Syracuse. Judge of his surprise to find his servant had slain his horse to prevent his return.

At Syracuse the hours of the afternoon were swiftly passing. The shadows began to lengthen along the valley of the Anapus, while those on the dial in the great square of the city darkened moment after moment, but Damon had not returned. As the sunset hour drew near, and still there were no signs of his appearance, no hastening horseman, no dust cloud on the distant hill-side, Pythias was led forth to execution. Dionysius was doubtless still more convinced that friendship was only words. Nothing daunted, with a still firm faith in the honor of his friend, Pythias ascended the scaffold, unterrified at the sight of the ax and block, the instruments of his now certain death.

The hour drew near. Out in the west the sun was sinking lower. Over in the east the shadows were climbing the walls of embattled Ortygia. A thin line of light, darkened on the dial, and a headless trunk and trunkless head would be all earth held of this brave soul.

But at this instant, dust-stained and breathless, Damon broke through the line of guards, and fell exhausted before the scaffold. It was a moment of intense joy to the rescued Pythias, and of intense surprise to the wondering tyrant. Pythias rejoiced, not that his friend had returned to suffer death, but that Damon's honor had been vindicated ; and the tyrant wondered at such devoted friendship and faithfulness to a pledged word in such trying circumstances. It was a new revelation of character to him. He could illy spare such men. Damon was pardoned at once, and Dionysius begged the privilege of being a third in that firm friendship of which he had seen such a convincing proof.

And this example did not spend its force that afternoon in Syracuse. There is something in the life and acts of a true man that is superior to time, that is and will be when time is no more. On such eternity is stamped. This is such an action. When men cease to admire true manliness, when the world has forgotten that its truest thing is a true life, when it is willing to tear out the pages of its history on which it has written its best, and noblest, and brightest deeds, then, and not till then, shall men cease to be moved by the story of Damon and Pythias.

It has been doubted whether this account of Damon and Pythias was not, like many of the other tales of the ancients, purely a fiction.   As often as this has been repeated, it is without the least warrant.   Grote, who has probably done most to destroy belief in the mythical Greek legends, and to give us a correct history of Greece, regards this story as well authenticated.   He says, " The story of the devoted attachment of the two Pythagoreans, Damon and Phintias, appears to be very well attested. Aristoxenus heard it from the lips of the younger Dionysius, the despot."   It will require something besides assertion to impugn such authority.

It should, however, be said, that though the main facts are as stated, in several minor matters, that do not in the least affect the story, there are some variations in the different accounts.   Phintias is probably the true name of one, instead of Pythias ; and, in some accounts, Damon is represented as taking the place of Phintias, instead of the opposite. The main facts are the same, however, in all versions.

We have thus briefly—far too much so, we fear—attempted to show what developed, in the lives of Damon and Pythias, such a glorious manifestation of friendship.   Out of all the Mysteries of the ancient world, Pythagoras gathered what was good, and fused it into one mass. Dust specks they came to him; massive gold they left his hand. He found, as he journeyed over the world, many of the deepest and divinest truths taught in these Societies. To these great truths he added one other, friendship. With an insight that seems almost a prophecy, he saw that the aim of all instruction on earth should be to bind men together. He taught not, as One afterward did, "That ye love one another," but he spoke of brotherly love as none other did for forty centuries of time. He dreamed of a coming age of gold, and his design was to hasten its coming. Virgil, borrowing from the Mysteries, sings of this age in a strain of sublime and lofty eloquence: "The last era of Cumæan song is now arrived. The great series of ages begins anew. Now, too, returns the virgin Astræa—returns the reign of Saturn. The serpent's sting shall die, and poison's fallacious plant shall die, and the Assyrian spikenard grow on every soil; and blushing grapes shall hang on brambles rude, and dewy honey from hard oaks distill; and fruits and flowers shall spring up every-where without man's care or toil. The sacred Destinies, harmonious in the established order of the Fates, will sing to their spindles, as they spin the mysterious

threads of life. 'Roll on, ye Golden Ages, roll!'"
In such a school were Damon and Pythias edu-
cated; in such hopes they lived, and from such
impulses they acted. Twice have a thousand years
passed since then, and what is the promise of the
hour? The age of gold has not come yet, but there
are earnest hearts praying for it, and earnest brains
toiling for it. Every one that bows with us about
an altar consecrated to true friendship is a positive
force to hasten its coming. We may not see its
dawn. "When this festal day comes, then will our
children's children be no more. We stand now in
the evening, and see, at the close of our dark day,
the sun go down with a red-hot glory, and promise,
behind the last cloud, the still, serene Sabbath-day
of humanity; but our posterity have yet to travel
through a night full of wind, and through a cloud
full of poison, till at last, over a happier earth, an
eternal morning-wind, full of blossom-spirits, moving on before the sun, expelling all clouds, shall
breathe on men without a sigh."[2]

Happy eyes, that shall see this morning! Happy
hearts, that shall feel its rapture! The sight and
rapture are not for us. We are born to the toil and
struggle.

[2] Jean Paul, Hesperus, Vol. I, 497.

PART II.

History of the Knights of Pythias.

Chapter IX.

Organization of the Knights of Pythias.

HERE have been certain hours in the world's history that have been especially fitted for the announcement of some great idea, for the inception of some great design. Nature and Providence always provide for the needs of the world. When that need is a present and pressing one, then it is met. And men's wants are supplied not much in advance. They are ever taught the lesson, "Take no thought for the morrow." They had lived on for ages satisfied with the means of communication that were furnished by wind and beast. But there came a time when men were no longer divided by barriers of hatred, when commerce and civilization had brought them into a closer union, and the old methods of communication were too slow. There was a call for something better, and the call was not in vain. The steamship, the railway, the telegraph, the cable, followed one another in rapid succession. When something better still is demanded, and mankind makes its draft upon Nature, it will not be dishonored.

But this principle holds true not only in regard to Nature, but in history as well. It is a deeply interesting study to look over the world's history and see how, when humanity was ready for some new idea, there has always been some one to think it and speak it. When the tale of bricks has grown burdensome, there has come to it some Moses to lead it from bondage to a land of promise. Luther, Cromwell, Napoleon, are names that come readily to mind in connection with these advances of humanity.

And it is to be observed, that the hours when humanity has struck its tents and sought new camping-grounds have been to all appearances strangely inopportune. It has been in the midst of overturnings and upheavals, when the very foundations of society seemed to be broken up, when with bit in teeth, and a loose rein, the world was dashing on to apparent destruction. Just at this hour some strong hand has grasped the reins, and a strong arm has curbed the raging world. Men have not seen this at the time. They have seen the toil and strife, the battle and the blood, the terrible sea before, and the still more terrible Egyptians behind, but the great deliverance is a thing which becomes great in its after results, not in its present accomplishments.

And we take it that the "KNIGHTS OF PYTHIAS" is just such a movement. It was founded at an hour that was loudly calling for a new proclamation of the well-nigh forgotten lessons of Friendship and Fraternity. We have not yet forgotten the hour. Its griefs are too fresh, its sorrows too deep, to have passed away. While we no longer cherish malice in the heart, yet, like some terrible dream, its scenes are often before us and always come with a shudder. One of the most baneful effects of our civil war was the sundering of all ties that had bound men together, the father from son, brother from brother. And this sundering was not only between those who were opposed to each other at the battle's front, but it extended to those who in political principles were joined. Greed seemed to be the god of the hour. For gain, men were bartering all that was true and pure. They had taken their holiest and dearest friendships and gone into the Babel mart, and bartered them away for gold. All was disunion, discord, anarchy, not only in the political world, but in men's hearts as well. It was an hour that had gone down into the depths of its sorrows, and was wailing loudly for some one with power to whisper to the world its holy lessons of Friendship, and lead men to Fraternity again.

And yet it seemed an hour the most unpromising for such a duty. Would men stop in the rush of business to hear of such things? With the pleasing clink of gold filling their ears, would they listen to the voice of Friendship? It was certainly unpromising, but the attempt was made.

Just how far the views we have advanced influenced the mind of the "Founder" of our Order, we can not tell, but it is very evident that their force must have impressed him. Whether they did or not, matters very little. The Order was what the hour needed, and he was only the instrument for meeting this need.

The idea of an Order, having for its main purpose the inculcation of lessons of Friendship, and based upon the old story of Damon and Pythias, seems to have originated with Brother P. S. C. J. H. Rathbone. There have been some questions in this connection that we have desired to have answered, but have failed to get replies to several letters we have sent to Brother Rathbone. It would be interesting to know what first suggested the idea, and the circumstances connected with the writing the Ritual. We hope these may be collected and given to the Order before it is too late.

The Ritual of the Initiatory, or, as it is now termed, the First Degree, having been written, several gentlemen were invited to meet at Temperance Hall, Washington, D. C., on the evening of the 19th February, 1864. The record of this meeting taken from the record book of Washington Lodge, No. 1, is as follows. We quote at second-hand from " THE KNIGHT'S ARMOR."

WASHINGTON, FEBRUARY 19, 1864.
At the Temperance Hall, Friday Evening.

" Upon agreement, a number of gentlemen met, and after some conversation upon the subject, they were called to order, and, upon motion of Mr. J. H. Rathbone, a chairman of the meeting was proposed, and Mr. J. T. K. Plant was unanimously called to the chair, and D. L. Burnett nominated as Secretary. After organizing as above, the object of the meeting was stated to be the organization or foundation of a society, its business and operations to be of a secret character, having for its ultimate object Friendship, Benevolence, and Charity. Before proceeding further, those present were requested to subscribe to an oath, laid down afterward in the Initiatory. All present having signified their willingness to do so, the same was administered to them, by reading the same by J. H. Rathbone. After taking the oath, on motion, it was resolved that this Order be styled the KNIGHTS OF PYTHIAS.

"On motion that a Committee be appointed to prepare a Ritual of opening and closing a Lodge, and of the ceremony of initiation into the same, the Chair appointed Brother J. H. Rathbone as said Committee, who immediately reported a Ritual, which he had prepared, and which, upon being read, was adopted. The Lodge then went into an election of officers, which resulted as follows:

Brother J. H. RATHBONE, Worthy Chancellor.
JOEL R. WOODRUFF, Vice-Chancellor.
J. T. K. PLANT, Venerable Patriarch.
D. L. BURNETT, Worthy Scribe.
A. VAN DERVEER, Banker.
R. A. CHAMPION, Assistant Banker.
GEORGE R. COVERT, Assistant Scribe.

"The Worthy Chancellor then appointed Brother M. H. Van DerVeer to be Worthy Guide, and A. Roderique as Inside Steward, and Brothers Kimball, Roberts, D. C., and W. H. Burnett to be Choral Knights. The Worthy Chancellor then appointed a Committee to prepare a Ritual for the first Degree (now the second), signs, etc., as follows: Brothers Kimball, Champion, and W. H. Burnett, and V. P. J. T. K. Plant, and W. C. J. H. Rathbone, as Chairman, added. Also, Committees to procure Regalia, etc., after which this, the first meeting of the Order, adjourned to meet again the evening of the 23d inst., to complete the organization."

Such was the beginning of the Knights of Pythias as an organization. Few, if any, present that Friday evening, in their wildest dreams, pictured its results. Doubtless some visions of success flashed before them, some prophecies of the work they could accomplish. They may have thought that in some *distant* day men might rise up and call them blessed ; that after they were dead, and others had taken their places, and worked out the ideas they had only drafted, their names would be as imperishable as those of Damon and Pythias ; but to think that in less than seven years one hundred thousand should listen to the story of that night with gratitude in their hearts, was something too wild and too daring to dream even ! But such is the reality—a reality that astonishes all calculations.

It will be noticed, from the Record we have given, that the Laws and Ritual differed in several respects from the one now in use. There have been changes made at various times, which will be noted in their proper place. At first the office of Venerable Patriarch was the *third*, instead of first as now; there were several offices which experience showed to be useless, as Assistant Scribe and Banker; the title of Scribe was afterward changed, and the office of Financial Scribe added.

The Committees appointed on the 19th went earnestly to work, and at the adjourned meeting on the 23d of February, were ready to report a Degree Ritual. This was subjected to a severe scrutiny and test and finally adopted, and the Committee discharged. The other Committees reported progress, and were continued.

Four days afterward, February 27th, the Lodge again met. The members, as well as the Committees, had been diligently at work, and several applications for membership were read and considered. A Committee was also appointed to prepare a Ritual for the second Degree—now the third—who reported a form at a subsequent meeting, which was adopted.

With the adoption of this Degree, the Lodge and

the Order were first fairly at work. The Brothers labored zealously ; good men and true were added to their numbers, and all seemed to promise the greatest success. On the 24th of March the first regular quarterly election was held, the regular officers were elected, and at the same time steps were taken to organize a Grand Lodge, and Brothers Woodruff, M. A. Van DerVeer, and Roderique were elected Representatives.

On the 8th of April following, these Representatives, with a sufficient number of Past Chancellors, from Washington Lodge, No. 1, met and organized the Grand Lodge of the District of Columbia, with Brother Joseph T. K. Plant as Grand Chancellor. A. Van DerVeer was elected Grand Scribe at the same time.

Two weeks after the organization of the Grand Lodge, Brother J. H. Rathbone resigned the office he held—that of Venerable Patriarch—and also his membership in the Order. The reason for this action does not appear, but it was probably dissatisfaction with the organization of the Grand Lodge. Up to this time the Venerable Patriarch was regarded as the third officer of the Lodge—from this time, in lists of officers, it always appears first. The Assistant Scribe and Banker were dispensed with.

Thus far but one Lodge was in existence. On the 12th of April, 1864, four days after the meeting of the Grand Lodge, Franklin Lodge No. 2 was instituted at the Navy Yard, Washington. This was an act second in importance to none that had thus far been done. The very life of our Order is the result of this institution. If Washington Lodge was the Mother Lodge, Franklin Lodge was its Foster-Mother, and when the former was dead, and could no longer give its child the care it needed, the latter nourished it with an affection as great, and a solicitude as deep, as though it gave it life and being. When that hour comes—as come it surely must—that our beloved Order has gone out into all the world on its mission of Friendship, Charity, and Benevolence, then shall men speak with a grateful reverence of the work Franklin Lodge has done. They will tell that when death stared us in the face, and men had gathered around to see us die, and were laughing at our death struggles, then this noble band of men took the dying Order to their hearts and warmed it into life again, and when its strength was restored, sent it forth on its glorious mission. Honor the men who gave our institution its being, but honor those with an equal honor who restored its life and power.

Its officers and members should be remembered. They were as follows at its institution:

    Rob't L. Middleton, Venerable Patriarch.

    Dan'l Carrigan, Worthy Chancellor.

    Edward Fox, Vice-Chancellor.

    Clarence M. Barton, Scribe.

    James Gill, Banker.

    Nicholas Watson, Guide.

    Jas. H. Lawrence, Inner Steward.

    Hudson Pettit, Outer Steward.

Edw'd Dunn, James W. Kelley, Jasper Scott, George Norton, and J. H. Wheeler, Charter Members.

Those of our Order who have followed its history will recognize familiar names, and will not wonder at the energy it displayed when for nearly eight months it was the only Lodge of the Order in the country. Of the five Past Supreme Chancellors reported in the last report, two are of this number.

The members of the Order worked bravely on, encouraged by this extension of its principles. The same rule, however, held true that always has since the world began. The Order was forced to endure the struggle with poverty. Indeed, it has always been so. Every movement of the world to a better

and purer life has been from want and poverty
Revolutions are always upward. But, nothing dis-
couraged, they worked on, and, though no one stood
near to prophesy of success, their own consciousness
was itself prophetic. On the 19th of May Columbia Lodge, No. 3, was formed, and June 2d Potomac Lodge, No. 4. This was the last Lodge
formed in 1864. Discouragements and trials were
at hand. That hour was coming that comes to
every person and every thing that is of any value,
the hour of severe testing, and as it comes out of
this hour, so will be its future life. Through the
Fall and Winter of this year, under the most discouraging circumstances, they struggled on. Early
in February a gleam of hope appeared, and a mo-
mentary joy came to the true Knights by its extension into Virginia. Brother John H. King, who was
in the United States Naval Service, and stationed at
Alexandria, succeeded on the 1st of February, 1865,
in establishing a Lodge at that place. This was
the first time the Order had gone beyond the city
of its birth, and for a moment roused the hope of
every Knight. Brother King was appointed Deputy
Grand Chancellor of Virginia, and great results
were expected.

But all these hopes were destined to disappointment. The coming of Spring, the uncertainty about every thing of a business nature, the high price of gold, and the constant changes taking place at the nation's capital, all worked against the Order. The finances of the Lodges were in a desperate condition, no revenue, and little prospect of any. In April Potomac and Columbia Lodges ceased to hold meetings, and Washington Lodge could hardly command a quorum. In July the Alexandria Lodge, after an existence of only three months, died out, and when the Grand Lodge met, but two Lodges were represented, namely, Washington and Franklin. At its session in June, 1865, the only business transacted was the election and installation of officers. On the 19th of this month the Grand Lodge held its last session under the existing forms, but one Lodge being represented. The next month Washington Lodge ceased to exist, its members in good standing being received by Franklin, which was now the only Lodge of the Order in existence. It was a dark hour, one that tested the firmness of the most hopeful, but this glorious band of true Knights toiled on and waited. This Lodge exercised all the duties of a Grand Lodge, installing their own officers, and working in every needed case as a Grand body.

At the close of 1865 Franklin Lodge had sixty members, and about two hundred dollars in the treasury. It was determined to make an effort to extend the Order by reviving the old Lodges and establishing new ones. Early in 1866 the Constitution was revised and printed, and on the 2d of April a committee was appointed by Franklin Lodge to canvass the City of Washington for a new Lodge. This was the beginning of a new era. After a sleep of eight months, the Order, with the return of Spring, warmed into life again.

This Committee soon reported fifteen names, and applied for a Charter to organize a new Lodge. This being granted by the Past Chancellors of Franklin Lodge, it at once begun work under the name of Mt. Vernon, No. 5.

There had been a long-felt need of some radical changes in both the Installation Service and the Ritual. About this time the former was revised, and, on the 30th of April, 1866, a committee was appointed to make the necessary changes in the latter. This Committee consisted of Past Chancellors Rathbone, Barton, Dunn, Cross, Cook, F. S. Lawson, and Brothers Cooksey, of Franklin Lodge, and F. S. Sears and V. P. Downs, of Mt. Vernon Lodge. They went diligently to work, and, on the

14th of May, 1866, reported the Ritual now in use, which differs materially from the old one, to a joint meeting of Franklin and Mt. Vernon Lodges. It was unanimously adopted, and with its adoption a new life of the Order began. The membership increased slowly, but the material was of the kind that promised permanence. It was at once resolved to revive the Grand Lodge, which had held no meetings since June, 1865, and make another effort under more favorable circumstances to spread the principles of the Order.

Here, properly, the first period in the history of the KNIGHTS OF PYTHIAS ends. For more than two years it had struggled along, now with the brightest prospects and then all but dead. But the trial was now over. The severe test of those eight long months, when but one Lodge held its meetings, and that with a constantly decreasing membership and a depleted treasury, had proved it, tried it, and it was not found wanting. The Order now took a new departure and began its wonderful course of triumph.

Chapter X.

Reorganization of the Knights of Pythias.

ARLY in May, 1866, the Committee appointed to resuscitate the Grand Lodge, consisting of Past Chancellors Rathbone, Barton, Dunn, King, Cook, and Beech, of Franklin Lodge, John S. Downes, and Representative Stromberger, of Mount Vernon Lodge, engaged in the task of reorganization. The action at this time was not only a re-establishment of the Grand Lodge, but an entire reorganization of the Order. During the month of April the Installation Service had been revised, new regalia proposed, and a new Ritual adopted. So, also, in the plan for the revival of the Grand Lodge, many changes were made. The offices of Grand Marshal, Herald, Prelate, and Inner and Outer Guardian, which existed at the time of the

156

decease of the Grand Lodge, the previous June, were abolished. The following officers were elected to fill out the unexpired term of those in office at the time the Grand Lodge became defunct:

J. H. RATHBONE, Grand Chancellor.
EDWARD DUNN, Vice Grand Chancellor.
CLARENCE M. BARTON, Grand Rec. Scribe.
JOHN S. DOWNES, Grand Financial Scribe.
JOHN H. KING, Grand Banker.
THOMAS W. COOK, Grand Guide.
LEVI BEECH, Grand Inner Steward.
JOHN W. CROSS, Grand Outer Steward.

At this meeting of the Grand Lodge, the venerable Grand Patriarch was made an appointed officer for three months, and the signs, grips, pass-words, etc., of the old work were changed by the G. C., and a secret cypher laid down. A committee was also appointed to have the Ritual printed, which was soon done.

At the next session of the Grand Lodge, May 28th, still further steps were taken to give permanence to the Order, and prevent a repetition of the dark days of '65 and '66. Committees were formed to draft a Constitution and By-Laws for the Grand Lodge, as well as to revise the Installation work;

also to secure charter and diploma designs for subordinate Lodges, and regalia for the Grand Lodge. From these proceedings the determination of the Brothers, and the prospect before them, may be readily inferred. The moment for retreat had passed, and all along the line rung out the cry, "Forward!" So impressed were the members with the idea that a new era had begun, that a proposition was made to declare null and void all the proceedings of the old Grand Lodge, and also to change the numbers of Franklin and Mount Vernon Lodges from 2 and 5 to Nos. 1 and 2. This was, however, wisely voted down. Though there were some things in the past which would willingly have been forgotten, still, in effacing these from the records, much that was good and dear to every Knight would also be destroyed. The struggles and efforts of the past had much that was glorious, and shed honor upon the little band that remained faithful. This history they could not well lose. In coming days it might serve the same purpose that the story of the trials of our fathers served—an incentive to nobler deeds and the proud boast of unnumbered ages.

But, while the numbers were allowed to remain the same, the fact is no different: Franklin Lodge is, in the best sense, FIRST.

So great was the amount of business to be performed, that sessions of the Grand Lodge followed each other in rapid succession. At an adjourned meeting, on the 4th of June, a form of application for new Lodges was presented by P. C. King and adopted. Franklin Lodge also delivered up all the property of the defunct Lodges, on the promise of payment of its cost, $18.75.

On the 18th of June the last session of the old Grand Lodge was held. The proceedings of this session were very important in their bearing on the future prosperity of the Order. The new Constitution and By-Laws were presented, and committees appointed. The financial condition was, however, as low as it could well be. There were but sixty-one dollars in the treasury, and, of this, sixty dollars was a loan. But there seems to have been not the least thought of discouragement. With circumstances none the brightest, the members displayed an energy that was truly surprising. It seems, indeed, as if courage was born out of obstacles. Indeed it always is. Terrors, nor frowns, nor indifference shook them. They needed all these to awake and fan their energies into a pure flame. Our Order was never quite itself until its life was put in peril, and then it showed its latent power.

This really ended the work of reorganization, though changes were afterward introduced, and committees had still to report. But from this moment there was no retrograde movement; every hour has added to its strength, and every day has gained it new victories.

Chapter XI.

Sessions of the Grand Lodge of the District of Columbia to the organization of the Supreme Lodge.

T is necessary to follow the history of the Grand Lodge of the District of Columbia with more minuteness than we shall that of other States, as almost every movement had an effect upon the Order generally. It was also, for a time, by virtue of its priority of origin, the head of the Order, and exercised the functions of a Provisional Supreme Lodge until a regular Supreme body was established.

The first session for the year 1866–67 was held July 9, 1866. Three new members from No. 5 presented their credentials, and were received as members of the Grand Lodge. The quarterly rè-turns showed a membership of only one hundred and thirty-nine, and an available fund of $334.70. Mt. Vernon Lodge was much the largest, nearly double that of Franklin, but was in no other respect its superior.

At this session new officers were elected, Brother Edward Dunn being Grand Chancellor, with an earnest body of men as his associates. The retiring Grand Chancellor for the first time succeeded to the office of Venerable Patriarch, which was now made the first office in the Lodge, instead of the third as heretofore. Brother J. H. Rathbone was thus the first Grand Venerable Patriarch under the new rule. The work of Alexandria Lodge was also purchased at this time by Brother P. C. John H. King, acting as committee for the Grand Lodge.

At a special session, held on the 12th of the same month, the printed Ritual was placed in the hands of a Committee of three, with instructions to compare it with the manuscript copies, and, if found correct, to destroy the original manuscripts. This the Committee did, corrected a few typographical errors, and destroyed the written ones. Every Lodge was ordered to deliver up the manuscript Ritual from which they had worked, and receive instead five of the printed ones.

On the 30th of July, at a special session, application was made for a Charter to open a new Lodge at the Navy Yard. The new Lodge was christened Liberty, No. 6, and started with forty-three members. The Charter was at once granted, and the members being in waiting, were introduced and initiated, and the officers installed.

This was a most encouraging sign, and inspired the members with a new hope. A joy, that, as we look at it now, seems almost extravagant, filled the hearts of the old members, and the Liberty Lodge was greeted with an enthusiasm such as had been extended to no others.

The Installation work for the Grand Lodge, which had been some time in preparation, was presented at a special session, August 8th, by P. G. C. Rathbone, and adopted. The Funeral service, with the addition of a short prayer, was also received as presented.

A little later, August 21st, a Charter was granted to Webster Lodge, No. 7, which was organized by the officers of the Grand Lodge on the 27th. A special session on the 7th of September closed the first quarter. There were now four Lodges in existence, but as yet the hard work of extending the Order had not begun, though every thing that seemed to promise success was done. The Ritual had been revised, regalia adopted, the price of supplies fixed, designs presented for Charters and diplomas, and every thing got in readiness for earnest work.

During the second quarter of this year, October to January, the regular quarterly and three special sessions were held. Various changes were made in the Constitution and By-Laws, and an entirely new Constitution for Subordinate Lodges was presented by P. C. Barton. After a careful consideration, at this and a subsequent meeting, it was adopted, and a Committee appointed to inquire into the expediency of printing it. It was also resolved, in view of the fact of his having been elected Grand Chancellor of the Order, in June, 1865, "that P. C. Clarence M. Barton be known hereafter as PAST GRAND CHANCELLOR of the Order."

There were no new Lodges instituted during the quarter, nor was the number of members greatly increased, the total being only fifty-five greater than at the close of the previous quarter. Yet they were of the best material. But better than all other signs was the spirit of inquiry concerning the Order that was rife, not only in the District, but in other States. These inquiries were frankly answered, and, instead of satisfying, only provoked a deeper interest in the minds of the inquirer, and an earnest desire to know more of what seemed to them of such worth. The interest in the middle States was especially noticeable, and an urgent and earnest demand came thence to know more of the objects, aims, and principles of the Knights of Pythias.

So the civil year drew to a close. At its commencement there was but one Lodge, with only sixty members. Now there were four, with about three hundred. The simple story of Damon and Pythias was working in power over the hearts of men and teaching its lessons of Friendship. The long course of preparation was almost at an end, and as loyal and leal Knights they were about to start on their chivalrous journey through the world, bound by the most solemn obligations to be true and good men, to succor the distressed, to speak hope to the disconsolate, to teach mankind its lessons of Fraternity, and above all, ever to be ready to do valiant battle for God and the Right.

The first session of the Grand Lodge for 1867 found a larger number of members present than ever before, and, with a heartiness inspired by their new-born hope, they greeted and congratulated each other on the glorious outlook of the New Year. They were not doomed to disappointment. After the usual routine business, and some new leg-

islation, the Grand Lodge adjourned to the 27th
of January. It was at this session of the Grand
Lodge, that we get the first sight of the destined
greatness of the Order. A fund had been privately
raised among the members to be expended in
establishing a Lodge in Pennsylvania, as soon as
an opportune moment should arrive. P. C. Hamilton announced the fact to the Grand Lodge, and
paid in the amount of the subscription. The G. C.
was at once authorized to pay over the money to
whoever was deputized to organize a Lodge outside
of the District. The details of the use of this
money, and of the establishment of the Order in
Pennsylvania, we reserve to a future chapter.

During the remainder of this Pythian year, the
Grand Lodge met often in quarterly and special
session. Steps were taken to resuscitate the dor-
mant Lodges, and bring them back into the Order.
The application of Excelsior Lodge, No. 1, Pennsylvania, was received, and a Charter granted; as was
also a Charter to organize a Lodge—Friendship, No.
8—in the south-western part of the City of Washington. Still later, and before the annual session,
a second Lodge was established in Philadelphia—
Keystone, No. 2. During the three months ending
with the 25th of June, the progress had been most

gratifying ; two hundred and twenty-four members had been initiated, and there was over $2,300 in the treasury, including a widows and orphans' fund of $574.13. At the last quarterly session previous to the annual, the Grand Lodge conferred the degree of Past Chancellor upon all the first installed officers of Excelsior Lodge, No. 1, of Philadelphia..

Previous to giving in detail the history of the Order in Pennsylvania, it may be as well to close our account of the actions of the Grand Lodge of the District of Columbia, previous to the formation of the Supreme Lodge.

The first meeting for the year '67–68 was opened July 23, 1867, with Grand Chancellor Edward Dunn in the chair. Application was received for a third Lodge in Philadelphia, permission granted to Keystone Lodge to keep its Charter open, and the officers for the ensuing year elected and installed.

During the quarter, no less than four special sessions were held, mainly for the purpose of acting upon applications for Charters from Pennsylvania. There is something wonderful in the progress the Order made in this State after it was once fairly in progress. It reads like a fairy story. The grand Pythian temple was rising in its beautiful proportions with a rapidity that made one believe genii were at work. And they were, not mythical ones, but the genii of Friendship, Charity, and Benevolence. During the quarter, ten Charters had been granted for Lodges in Pennsylvania—all but one, which was at Reading, being in Philadelphia. At the beginning of July, 1867, the total membership was six hundred and ninety-four. At the end of the quarter it was two thousand and twenty-four—a net increase in three months of one thousand three hundred and thirty. The total fund on hand amounted to $4,712.27. During this quarter, Franklin Lodge, No. 2, District of Columbia, made an application for a regular Charter in place of the dispensation under which it had been working since April 12, 1864. This was, of course, at once granted as a simple act of justice.

At a meeting of the Grand Lodge, held October 8th, a petition was received from Pennsylvania, praying for a Charter for a Grand Lodge for that State. After considerable discussion a Charter was granted, to take effect on, or about, January 1, 1868, and in the mean time a dispensation was issued to them as a Grand Lodge *pro tem*. One half of the percentage paid by the Lodges in Pennsylvania during this and the succeeding quarters, was also ordered to be returned.

The present badge, consisting of a helmet, shield, ax, spear, etc., encircled by a ring, and bearing the letters F. C. B., was presented by P. C. Coppes, of Excelsior, No. 1, of Philadelphia, and adopted.

During this time, the Grand Lodge, being the oldest, exercised all the rights and privileges of a Supreme Lodge, granting Charters to both Grand and Subordinate bodies, and claiming the right of supervision until a Supreme Lodge could be organized. Charters were rapidly issued to form other Lodges in Pennsylvania. At the session of November 27th, Golden Lodge, No. 1, and Monumental Lodge, No. 2, Baltimore, Maryland, were chartered, and on the 10th of the following month, to these were added two in New Jersey, four in Pennsylvania, and one in District of Columbia. For a full account of these, we refer to our chapters on the origin and progress of the Order in these States.

15

Chapter XII.

Origin and Progress of the Order in Pennsylvania, Maryland, New Jersey, and Delaware.

S we have already stated, at the session of the Grand Lodge of the District of Columbia, held September 7, 1866, P. C. Hamilton announced the gratifying fact that a sum of money had been subscribed and paid for the purpose of organizing Lodges outside of the District. At a meeting on the 12th of February, the following year, as we learn from "THE KNIGHT'S ARMOR," "After the transaction of all the business before the Grand Lodge, P. G. C. Barton, in a short speech, stated that he had for some time been in correspondence with gentlemen in Philadelphia, touching the objects of the Order, and the question of establishing a Lodge in that city, and from the tenor of those letters, believed that the Order would meet with a cordial reception there from many good men who were anxious to avail themselves of the opportunities afforded by the Order to do good unto others. He asked for an appropriation of money to defray expenses of a visit to Philadelphia."

The sum of $20 was appropriated amid the wildest enthusiasm, and, in the event of the success of his mission, Past Chancellors Rathbone, Dunn, Cross, and Carrigan were deputized to assist in forming the new Lodge.

Three days after, P. G. C. Barton was in Philadelphia, where he consulted with those with whom he had corresponded, and met them at the residence of one of their number in the north-western part of the city. Arrangements were made for a meeting on the 19th, at the house of George Henslee, corner of Fifteenth and Brown streets, for the purpose of organizing a Lodge. Mr. Henslee was chosen chairman, and Brother Barton explained the principles and objects of the Order. All present subscribed to an application for a Charter, and named as their officers:

WILBUR H. MYERS, Venerable Patriarch.
FRED. COPPES, Worthy Chancellor.
JOHN J. FISHER, Worthy Vice-Chancellor.
WILLIAM A. PORTER, Worthy Banker.

A. J. HUHLZINGER, Worthy Financial Scribe.

G. GROSS, Worthy Recording Scribe.

J. W. HENCILL, Worthy Guide.

JAMES M. DEVITT, Worthy Inside Steward.

Joined to this were nineteen names besides those of the officers.

The application was received by the Grand Lodge of the District of Columbia, and at once acted upon, and the Charter granted. It has been one of the great secrets of the success of the Knights of Pythias, that they have lost no time in dallying and useless delays. To resolve has been to act. Arrangements were made to proceed to Philadelphia, Saturday, the 23d of February, and organize the Lodge. It was a marked act, a white-letter day in the history of the Order, and the brethren determined to show their appreciation of it. On the morning of the 23d, the Committee appointed to go to Philadelphia and assist Brother Barton, was escorted to the depot from Mt. Vernon Lodge-room by the different Lodges, headed by Heald's band.

"The Committee were received in Philadelphia by Brothers Barton and Dunn, and the members of Excelsior Lodge, No. 1, and conducted to the Hall of the Mechanic Fire-Engine Company, Brown-street, below Fifteenth, where, at 8 o'clock, P. M.,

on the same day, they organized a Lodge and installed the officers."

It is impossible to overestimate the result of the
introduction of the Order into Pennsylvania. Previous actions and previous movements had doubtless placed the KNIGHTS OF PYTHIAS on a firm
basis, and made the possibility of the recurrence
of the dark days of '65 a remote one at least. But
as yet, it had only been preparing for the work that
was before it. It had mustered its forces, matured
its plan of attack, and waited for the opportune moment to advance. It came, and with that certainty
that seems akin to an inspiration, the right thing
was done at the right time. The little band of men
at the nation's capital, who had stood firm in the
darkest hour, felt a glow of enthusiasm in their
hearts, and heard a voice speaking to their consciousness of the brilliant future, and with a re-
newed zeal they labored on.

The work at once began in Pennsylvania, of extending our glorious principles. At the session of
the Grand Lodge of the District of Columbia, July
9, 1867, an application was made by Excelsior
Lodge to make all their first officers Past Chancellors, which petition was at once granted. Six days
after, KEYSTONE LODGE, No. 2, Philadelphia, sent

up an application for a Charter, bearing date June 29, 1867, with twenty-six names. The following Thursday, P. C. Kronheimer instituted the Lodge, and installed its officers. These were but drops before the shower. The following list will give some idea of the rapidity of the work. The dates are those appended to the applications.

CHOSEN FRIENDS LODGE, No. 3, July 20, 1867.
QUAKER CITY LODGE, No. 4, July 31st.
FRIENDSHIP LODGE, No. 5, Reading, August 3d.
STAR OF BETHLEHEM LODGE, No. 6, August 12th.
ADELPHIA LODGE, No. 7, August 17th.
DAMON LODGE, No. 8, August 24th.
APOLLO LODGE, No. 9, September 6th.
SPARTA LODGE, No. 10, September 7th.
LIBERTY LODGE, No. 11, September 9th.

All of these, with the exception of No. 5, were in Philadelphia, making an increase of ten Lodges during the quarter.

At the session of the Grand Lodge, October 8, 1867, the report from Pennsylvania showed eleven Lodges, and an aggregate membership of ELEVEN HUNDRED, the result of about six months' labor.

Believing that the interests of the Order would be advanced by establishing a Grand Lodge in their own State, the Lodges in the Keystone State sent in a petition at this session asking for power to do so. As we have already stated, this petition elicited considerable discussion, but the prayer of the petitioners was granted and a Charter ordered to be issued to take effect about January 1, 1868. Until that time they were empowered to work under a dispensation. At this same session half the percentage paid by the Lodges in Pennsylvania during this and the previous quarter, was ordered to be paid to the new Grand Lodge, that they might begin on a firm financial basis.

The Order increased so rapidly, that it was not thought best to adhere to the original programme. On the 10th of December there were thirty-one Lodges in the State, as many as ten having been organized in one week. In view of this rapid increase, it was decided to organize the Grand Lodge at once. On the 13th of December, 1867, the officers of the Provisional Supreme Lodge, with forty-five members, arrived in Philadelphia for this purpose.

They were received by the officers of the Grand and Subordinate Lodges, and moved in procession through the principal streets to the quarters provided for them. "The wildest enthusiasm prevailed among the members, hundreds of whom had closed their places of business with a view of making a gala day of the occasion."

The installation services took place in the evening, at the American Mechanics' Hall, corner of Fourth and George. Upward of *two thousand* members were present. Grand Chancellor Westwood presided, conveying the greetings of the Grand Lodge, District of Columbia, to the one about to be organized, and after prayer by the V. G. P. Edward Dunn, duly installing the following officers:

WILBUR H. MYERS, Venerable Grand Patriarch.
FRED. COPPES, Grand Chancellor.
GEO. W. CROUCH, Vice Grand Chancellor.
WM. BLANCBOIS, Grand Recording Scribe.
WM. S. SLOCUM, Grand Financial Scribe.
WM. S. ROSE, Grand Banker.
C. B. PRENTISS, Grand Guide.
JOS. L. NICHOLS, Grand Inner Steward.
EDWIN T. MARTIN, Grand Outer Steward.

The occasion was enlivened by the presentation of several very appropriate tokens of Friendship and of appreciation of services. Grand Chancellor Coppes was the recipient of a magnificent black velvet apron Regalia, which was presented to him in a very happy speech by P. G. C. Clarence M. Barton. The reply was equally felicitous. Grand Guide C. B. Prentiss, on behalf of Damon Lodge, No. 8, presented two splendid silver pitchers and salvers to P. G. C. Clarence M. Barton and P. G. C. Wilbur H. Myers.

After the installation ceremonies, the Grand Lodge, and all the members of the Order present, partook of a splendid banquet, spread at the Washington House. The visiting brothers were entertained for two days in that generous style that Philadelphia is so famous for, and then left for Washington with the liveliest recollections of their stay, and a high opinion of the hospitality of Pennsylvania Knights.

MARYLAND.

It was simply an impossible thing for the principles of Pythian friendship to spread from the District of Columbia, across the State of Maryland, into Pennsylvania, without the good people of that State being more or less moved regarding the objects of the Order. A spirit of inquiry took possession of not a few in different parts of the State, and in Baltimore particularly, which finally led to the formation of a Lodge, a call for proper officers

to initiate them, and then followed a prompt application for a Charter for Golden Lodge, No. 1, Baltimore, quickly followed by Monumental Lodge, No.
2, of the same place, both of which were granted by
the Grand Lodge, District of Columbia, Washington, November 27, 1867.

The officers and members of these two Lodges
immediately commenced a rigid study of the duties
devolving upon themselves ; learning which, they
set to work faithfully to perform them.   The field
before them was ample and inviting, promising a
rich return for labor bestowed.   The little band
made their influence felt throughout the city, in the
many acts of friendship toward each other in their
daily avocations, by their prompt attendance at
their Lodge meetings, and strict observance of obligations.   At the first regular quarterly session of
the Grand Lodge, District of Columbia, for the year
1868, held January 28th, application for a Charter
for Baltimore City Lodge, No. 3, was made, in proper
form, accompanied by the Charter fee, and the requisite number of signatures.   It was granted with
promptness, and a blessing on the cause in the
State was invoked.   This was followed by another
from De Haven Lodge, No. 4, Baltimore, at a special
session, held March 10, 1868, which was granted

in the same prompt manner the former ones were. It was at this session that the Grand Lodges of New Jersey and Maryland applied for Charters, which were granted. The Grand Lodge of Maryland was organized, with four Subordinate Lodges, each of which labored assiduously to advance the Order in the State. The application for the Grand Lodge Charter was signed by the following named Past Chancellors : N. M. Bowen, O. C. Wrigley, C. F. Abbott, W. H. Tindle, John Burns, G. G. Grun, F. Turner, W. Baxter, John Orem, W. P. Espey, Charles E. Lowe, and James A. Campbell. G. C. W. P. Westwood, assisted by P. C. John Shelley, of the District of Columbia, and several of the above-named P. C.'s of Maryland, opened the Grand Lodge in due form. After conferring the Grand Lodge Degree upon P. C.'s F. Turner, No. 2 ; William P. Espey, No. 2 ; William Baxter, No. 2 ; and O. C. Wrigley, No. 1, the officers elect of the Grand Lodge were installed as follows :

> JAMES A. CAMPBELL, Grand Chancellor.
> C. F. ABBOTT, Grand Vice-Chancellor.
> F. TURNER, Grand Recording Scribe.
> N. M. BOWEN, Grand Banker.
> CHARLES E. LOWE, Grand Guide.
> W. P. ESPEY, Grand Inner Steward.

The Grand Financial Scribe, G. G. Green, and the
Grand Outer Steward, John Orem, were not present at the installation.   After the organization was
complete, the Grand Lodge proceeded, in a busi-
ness-like manner, to deal with all questions before
it ; appointing standing committees, etc.   The Subordinate Lodges were stimulated to greater exertions, and exhorted to labor without ceasing, by the
example set them by their Grand Lodge officers.

The Grand Lodge held a special session April 7,
1868, and granted Charters to two Subordinate
Lodges—Good Intent, No. 6, and Damon, No. 5—
both of which were instituted the following week.
At the first regular quarterly session held April
28th, the Grand Lodge was informed that the same
action was taken in regard to dues as in the case
of Pennsylvania.   This action of the P. S. Lodge
was timely indeed, and gave the Order in Maryland
a good helping hand, at a time when the assistance
was most needed.

At the special session of the Grand Lodge, held
June 2, 1868, a charter was granted Excelsior
Lodge, No. 8, Baltimore, the application for which
was signed by eleven Knights of the Order, and a
long list of names of citizens desiring to become
members.   The deepest interest in the Order was

felt by all who were philanthropically inclined, and the need of something better than the common ties of mutual interest, to induce people to cultivate principles of true friendship toward each other. With this feeling among the better class of the business community throughout the State of Maryland, the Order could but prosper. The story is told by the Grand Chancellor, in his first annual report, at the first session of the Grand Lodge, held January 26, 1869, in the following words :

"It is needless for me to call attention to the rapid growth of our noble Order. With a member·ship of less than two hundred and fifty a year ago, we now number over twenty-five hundred ; and the large amount of labor which must necessarily have been bestowed by the officers, committees, and members of this body, will be apparent to you. Some of them have labored night and day, even to the neglect of their families and business, and have triumphed over opposition and prejudice. I feel I can safely say that, as an Order, our success has been unprecedented."

These words were amply supported by the facts. There were reported at the first annual session, held January 26, 1869, in the city of Baltimore, twenty-five Lodges of the Order, with an aggregate membership of two thousand five hundred, whose financial condition was as follows:

Amount on hand	. . . . . .	$2,929 51
Total receipts	. . . . . .	10,790 49
Percentage to Grand Lodge	. . . .	909 03
Expended for relief of Brothers	. . . .	196 08
Expenditures	. . . .	5,975 84
Orphans and Widows' fund	. . . .	2,055 90
Amount on hand and invested	. . .	7,778 49

The steady growth of the Order since that date has in no wise diminished, but continues to cheer the Brotherhood with its promises of spreading its benign influence to every village and town in the State. There have been trials, and some very severe ones, but they have related, for the most part, to matters of government. The principles have ever remained the same, and while there have been desperate efforts made to overrule some commands of the Supreme Lodge, the glorious foundation of our Order has remained unshaken.

NEW JERSEY.

Across the Delaware from Pennsylvania, over in the gallant little State of New Jersey, a deep interest in the Order had been awakened by the silent influence of the principles of true Pythian Friendship and Brotherly Love, which was seen and felt wherever the members of the Order had visited. During the Fall of 1867, several gentlemen in various parts of the State expressed a strong desire to know more of the Knights of Pythias Order, but delayed action, hoping some one more energetic than themselves would bring it into the State, and enable them to test its merits.

This State of things existed until November of that year, when parties in Camden and Mount Holly, each ignorant of the movements of the other, determined to form a Lodge, and apply for a Charter. In Camden, nine members of the I. O. O. F. resolved to go over to Philadelphia, join the Order, if possible investigate thoroughly its principles, objects, etc., and if found to be what was claimed for it, immediately transplant it to the genial soil of New Jersey. The gallant nine were elected members, and initiated in Philadelphia with due solemnity. They were delighted with the practical lessons there taught, and immediately drew their cards. On the next day, the 29th of November, they organized Damon Lodge, No. 1, of New Jersey, and petitioned for a Charter, which petition, with the Charter fee, was forwarded to the Grand Lodge, District of Columbia. Notwithstanding this, haste, several gentlemen in Mount Holly, Burlington county, New Jersey, were one day in advance, they having applied for a Charter on the 28th, the day before. Upon being informed of this fact, Damon Lodge changed her number to 2, and received her Charter, as did New Jersey Lodge, No. 1, also. On the 12th of December, the Grand Officers of the Grand Lodge, District of Columbia, assisted by the officers of the Grand Lodge of Pennsylvania, installed New Jersey Lodge, No. 1, of Mount Holly, and Damon Lodge, No. 2, of Camden, at Odd Fellows' Hall, in the latter city.

The new Lodges immediately set to work to build up the Order in their respective localities, and to extend it into other cities throughout the State.

The Provisional Supreme Lodge, in session in Washington, District of Columbia, December 31st, received an application for a Charter from St. Chrysostom Lodge, No. 3, dated Newark, New Jersey, December 23, 1867, which was granted.

Also, at the adjourned special session, was granted a Charter to Excelsior Lodge, No. 4, dated Bridgeton, N. J., December 30, 1867.

Also, at the same session, a Charter for Chester Lodge, No. 5, dated Moorestown, N. J., January 3, 1868.

At the next regular quarterly session, held January 28th, a Charter for Ivanhoe Lodge, No. 6, dated Millville, N. J., January, 1868, was granted, in answer to an application for the same.

In special session, March 10, 1868, the Provisional Supreme Lodge granted a Charter to establish a Grand Lodge of the Order in the State of New Jersey, and, at the same time, a Charter for Forrest Lodge, No. 7, Salem, N. J., which completed the number of subordinate Lodges in this State up to the time of the organization of the Grand Lodge, March 16, 1868.

Immediately after the formation of Nos. 1 and 2, Samuel Read, Esq., of Mount Holly, was appointed Deputy Grand Chancellor of the State, by the Grand Chancellor of the Grand Lodge, District of Columbia, and of the Provisional Supreme Lodge, by virtue of the power vested in him by the Constitution. Damon Lodge, No. 2, of Camden, protested against this appointment, claiming that he had "never presided over a single meeting of his Lodge."

The protest was referred to a committee, who reported, sustaining the appointment as legal, just, and proper.

At the organization of the Grand Lodge, Deputy Grand Chancellor Read was elected Grand Chancel-

16

lor for the first term.   The following were the Grand Lodge officers elected at that time:

ROB'T T. S. HEATH, Grand Venerable Patriarch.
SAMUEL READ, Grand Chancellor.
ROBERT MUFFITT, Vice Grand Chancellor.
WM. B. FRENCH, Grand Recording Scribe.
CHARLES W. HEISLER, Grand Financial Scribe.
ANTHONY PHILLIPS, Grand Banker.
JOHN T. TOMPKINS, Grand Guide.
JOHN L. SHARP, Grand Inner Steward.
FRED. L. COBB, Grand Outer Steward.

On the very day of the organization and installation of the Grand Lodge, it granted a Charter to Morning Light Lodge, No. 8, at Newport, and, on April 20th, granted Charters to the following:

Mariola Lodge, No. 9, Woodbury; Spartacus Lodge, No. 10, Trenton; Nonpareil Lodge, No. 11, Camden; Hadden Lodge, No. 12, Haddenfield; and from July 20, 1868, to March 18, 1869, eight others were granted.

The Order has made quite steady progress in this State since its first introduction, giving encouragement to the Brotherhood beyond her borders by her cordial welcome to its principles.   Its membership have been especially active in their efforts to extend the Order. It is to the exertions of G. C. Samuel Read mainly that so many States have brought their offerings to the Pythian Temple, and laid them upon the shrine of Friendship.

DELAWARE.

At the adjourned special session of the Grand Lodge, D. C., held January 7, 1868, an application for a Charter for Washington Lodge, No. 1, Wilmington, Delaware, dated December 31, 1867, was made, numerously signed by some of the best citizens of that city. The Charter was granted, the Lodge was organized, and the officers and members instructed thoroughly in the mysteries of the degrees, on the 13th day of January, by the Grand Chancellor, William P. Westwood, Grand Guide, H. Kronheimer, of the Grand Lodge, D. C., and William Blancbois, Grand Recording Scribe, of Pennsylvania. The Order was received cordially, and the Grand Officers welcomed in their midst by the members of the Order and citizens, who called on Past Chancellor Edwin Hirst, of Washington Lodge, No. 1, to inquire whether or not a new Lodge could be formed in a place where a Lodge already ex-'isted, without members from any previously existing

Lodge—which question Past Chancellor Hirst sub
mitted to the Grand Chancellor, who returned answer
that "citizens have the right to form new Lodges
anywhere, even though other Lodges may exist there
at the time; and that there was no law requiring
Brothers to withdraw from their Lodge to form new
ones."

With this assurance from the highest authority
in the Order, several of the good citizens organized
a new Lodge, and applied to the Grand Lodge,
D. C., through Past Chancellor Edwin Hirst, for a
Charter for Lafayette Lodge, No. 2, Wimington,
Delaware, with fee and requisite number of signatures inclosed, which the Grand Lodge granted,
and instructed Deputy Grand Chancellor Edwin
Hirst to institute the new Lodge and install the
officers:

> JAMES E. REYNOLDS, Venerable Patriarch.
> JOHN WRIGHT, Worthy Chancellor.
> ROBERT WHITE, Vice Chancellor.
> AQUILLA NEBEKER, Recording Scribe.
> SAMUEL H. CLOUD, Financial Scribe.
> ABNER E. BAILEY, Banker.
> HENRY M. LEWIS, Guide.
> JEROME B. CLARKE, Inner Steward.
> FERDINAND CHAIRS, Outer Steward.

On the 8th of February a Charter was granted to Lincoln Lodge, No. 3, Wilmington, Delaware, and instructions to institute the Lodge and install the officers, sent to D. G. C. Hirst; also, at a later date, to Clayton Lodge, No. 4.

An application was made to the Provisional Supreme Lodge, for a Charter for the Grand Lodge of Delaware, dated April 29, 1868, Wilmington, Delaware, signed by Past Chancellor Edwin Hirst, L. Bibley, James L. Smith, R. Rigby, No. 1; Past Chancellors James E. Reynolds, James Wright, Robert White, J. P. Hayes, No. 3; Past Chancellors R. P. Gacey, H. S. Truitt, and E. L. Seeley, of No. 4, with the seal of the four subordinate Lodges attached. The prayer of the petitioners was unanimously granted, and the Grand Lodge soon after instituted, and the officers installed. From this date the Order commenced a rapid growth in the State, equaling the expectations of the most sanguine of its members. Its principles have a firm footing there, and the Order will become a fixture in the catalogue of benevolent institutions in Delaware.[1]

We have now finished our account of the organization of all the Grand Lodges that existed at the

[1] For most of this chapter we are indebted to THE KNIGHT'S ARMOR, and in this manner confess our obligation.

time of the formation of the Supreme Lodge.   The
Order was now on a firm foundation, and nothing but
the most willful criminality could injure it.   It was
destined to undergo a severer test than any that it
had yet experienced, and one that, as we write, has
not yet passed ; but its foundations are too deep,
and the superstructure too massive, to be overthrown.
Our founders, in the dark days, like those of Emerson's grand poem,

"Builded better than they knew;"

and we, in the days to come, shall build yet

"More stately mansions."

Chapter XIII

Organization of the Supreme Lodge of the World.

HE Order was growing in strength every day, far surpassing in its vigor all the hopes that its truest friends had entertained. Almost every mail brought to Washington some new surprise for the officers of the Provisional Supreme Lodge. From distant parts of the country where there was no reason for supposing that the name even had penetrated, came not only requests for information concerning the Order, but applications for Charters. In five States and Districts Grand Lodges had been instituted, and in three others, Louisiana, New York, and Virginia, Subordinate Lodges were at work. This state of affairs loudly called for some more responsible head for the Order. Accordingly, at the session of the

Grand Lodge of the District of Columbia, G. R. S.
Clarence M. Barton introduced a series of resolutions looking to the formation of a Supreme Lodge.
The design was set forth in the first resolution,
which read as follows:

Be it Resolved, That the Grand Recording Scribe
be directed to notify the Grand Lodges of Pennsylvania, Maryland, and New Jersey to elect ten delegates for the purpose of meeting in joint Convention
to recommend to the Grand Lodges some definite
plan of forming the Supreme Lodge of the United
States.

Before the Convention met, Delaware had been
added to the list of Grand Lodges, and this State
also sent delegates.

The various Grand Bodies immediately upon receipt of information concerning the action of the
Grand Lodge of the District of Columbia, at once
took action.   Delegates were appointed, and, on the
15th of May, 1868, the Convention met in Commercial Lodge-room, in the Southwark Hose-house,
on Third-street, Philadelphia.

The five Grand Lodges were fully represented,
and at 10 o'clock the Convention was called to
order by William P. Westwood, Grand Chancellor
of the Provisional Supreme Lodge.   It appears

from the report of the Committee on Credentials, that every delegation was full, fifty delegates being present. The following were elected by acclamation as permanent officers :

President—WM. BLANCBOIS, of Pennsylvania.
Vice-Presidents—SAMUEL READ, of New Jersey ;
     N. M. BOWEN, of Maryland ;
     JAMES P. HAYES, of Delaware.
Secretary—CLARENCE M. BARTON, of District of
 Columbia.

After the usual preliminaries, a committee was appointed to present a plan for organizing the Supreme Lodge. A plan was at once reported, which, after being amended, was adopted. It was as follows:

The Supreme Lodge shall be composed of Past Grand Chancellors, and three Representatives from each Grand Lodge, their election as such making them Past Grand Chancellors. They shall be elected for two years, at the same meeting at which the deliberations of this Convention are ratified.

They shall meet in Supreme Lodge in the City of Washington, District of Columbia, upon the second

Tuesday in August, 1868, and proceed to organize by electing a

> Founder and Supreme Past Chancellor.
> Supreme Venerable Patriarch.
> Supreme Chancellor.
> Supreme Vice-Chancellor.
> Supreme Recording and Corresponding Scribe.
> Supreme Banker.
> Supreme Guide.
> Supreme Inner Steward.
> Supreme Outer Steward.

The said body, after organizing as above, shall be hailed, and known, and recognized as the Supreme Authority of the Knights of Pythias of the world.

All the present officers of the State Grand Lodges are declared Past Grand Chancellors.

> Respectfully submitted.
>
> WM. BLANCBOIS,

Attest: *President of the Convention.*

> CLARENCE M. BARTON, *Sercetary.*

This was at once transmitted to the Grand Lodges represented, for their action. The Grand Lodge of the District of Columbia ratified it at its session of June 8th. The Past Grand Chancellors and Representatives were notified to meet at Washington on the 11th of August, 1868. They were promptly on hand, and were called to order by William Blanc-bois, President of the Convention. At the election, which was the first order of business, the various offices were filled as follows :

J. H. RATHBONE, (D. C.,) Past Supreme Chancellor and Founder.

WILBUR H. MYERS, (Penn.,) Supreme Venerable Patriarch.

SAMUEL READ, (N. J.,) Supreme Chancellor.

J. P. HAYES, (Del.,) Supreme Vice-Chancellor.

C. M. BARTON, (D. C.,) Supreme Recording and Corresponding Scribe.

WM. A. PORTER, (Penn.,) Supreme Banker.

C. F. ABBOTT, (Md.,) Supreme Guide.

H. KRONHEIMER, (Penn.,) Supreme Inner Steward.

FRED. COPPES, (Penn.,) Supreme Outer Steward.

By vote P. G. C. William P. Westwood, who had been Grand Chancellor of the Provisional Supreme Lodge, was declared to be a Past Supreme Chancellor. On taking the chair, S. C. Samuel Read returned thanks for the honor in an able speech, when, after thanking the President of the Convention, William Blancbois, for the able manner in which he discharged his duties, the Supreme Lodge adjourned until afternoon.

At the afternoon session a petition was presented from certain ladies in Philadelphia, praying that a Charter might be granted them, with such rights and privileges as the Supreme Lodge might direct. As no provision had been made for such a Lodge, the petition was not granted. The subject has been revived several times since. At the meeting of the Supreme Lodge in 1870, an attempt was made to institute a degree of Ruth, for ladies. A ritual, which had been prepared, was presented and referred to a Committee, who reported favorably, but the adoption of such a degree was rejected. An effort is being made now to compass its adoption, with what success remains to be seen. Should it be successful, the question of the propriety of a different name, more in keeping with the names of the other degrees, would arise.

After adopting laws for the government of Subordinate Lodges, and transacting business of minor importance, the Supreme Lodge adjourned to meet in Wilmington, Delaware, on the 9th of November, 1868.

It will be necessary for us to hasten on to the First Annual Session of the Supreme Lodge, which was opened at Covenant Hall, Richmond, Virginia, March 9, 1869. Representations were present from New York, New Jersey, Pennsylvania, Delaware, Maryland, Virginia, District of Columbia, and Connecticut. The reports of the Supreme Chancellor and Supreme Scribe showed a very flattering condition of affairs. The Order had been introduced into twelve States, and others stood ready to receive it. Grand Lodges had been organized in New York, Virginia, and Connecticut, in addition to the five that assisted in organizing the Supreme Lodge. The returns showed a membership of over thirty-five thousand, nearly two hundred Lodges, and an income of $194,573.25. A condition of things like this was not only gratifying, but inspiring. The Supreme Lodge went to work with the utmost energy, determined that nothing should be left undone that could advance the interests of the Order.

An application was received early in the session from certain colored citizens of Philadelphia, praying that they might be " permitted to have and enjoy the great privileges and benefits of the Knights of Pythias." The Committee to whom the petition was referred reported :

" In reference to an application from a number of colored gentlemen from Philadelphia for a Charter, your Committee can not recommend its adoption, as we deem it entirely inexpedient to take any action on it at present, for many and obvious reasons."

This report called forth an earnest debate, some of the ablest members strongly urging the granting of a Charter, and others equally as able opposing it. On the call of the house the yeas and nays stood twenty-four to thirteen, and the report of the Committee was adopted, and the Charter refused.

At this session the Grand Chancellors of the Grand Lodge of District of Columbia, who had served previous to the organization of the Supreme Lodge, were declared to be Past Supreme Chancellors. To these were added P. G. C. W. H. Myers. They were ranked as follows:

1. Jos. S. K. Plant.
2. Clarence M. Barton.
3. Justus H. Rathbone.
4. Edward Dunn.
5. W. P. Westwood.
6. Wilbur H. Myers.

Brother Rathbone subsequently resigned his position, so that in the reports only five appear.

A Charter was granted to Steuben Lodge, No. 1, of Ohio, adding another to the list of States. Per-

mission was given the Supreme Chancellor to make
Knights at sight, whenever in his judgment the
interests of the Order would be advanced. Several
Brothers who had been instrumental in extending
the Order were declared to be Past Grand Chancellors. There were also at this session an unusual
number of appeals presented and disposed. The
lack of any decisions in doubtful points made it
difficult for officers to decide. This was a fault,
however, that was to be expected, and was received
as a matter of course. The Supreme Lodge adjourned on the evening of March 11, 1869, to meet
in New York, the second Tuesday in March, 1870.

Chapter XIV.

Supreme Lodge, Session of 1870.

PRECISELY at the time stated, 10, A. M., March 8, 1870, the Supreme Lodge was called to order by Supreme Chancellor Read. The report of the Committee on Credentials showed a representation from sixteen States. The prosperity of the past year had been unparalleled. From eight Grand Lodges the number had increased to sixteen, with Lodges in nine other States, making twenty-five States in which the Order had been planted. The number of Lodges had increased to four hundred and sixty-five, and of members to over fifty-two thousand. The finances were also in a healthy condition, the total receipts being $541,219.34. From the new Grand Lodges came members burning with zeal for the success and extension of the Order; but, as they clasped hands with their elder Brethren, and looked them in the eye, they saw a determination none the less, and an interest in no way inferior to their own.

Business was at once commenced. The reports of the Supreme Chancellor and Scribe were read, and referred to the appropriate Committees. The business transacted was, for the most part, routine, hearing appeals, deciding requests for honorary degrees, reception of reports, and other business of a like character.

There is one matter, however, that has had such an influence upon our Order that we must give the action more in detail, though we could wish it were not necessary to mention it. We refer to the Conclaves of S. P. K., and the adoption of the O.B.N. Though, as a member of the Order, we have our individual opinion, as is our right, we do not believe that, in a work like this, which is designed for general circulation, we have any right to intrude that opinion. We wish it to be understood, then, that any thing we shall state is to be regarded as a matter of history, and not as an expression of opinion.

For a clear understanding of the matter, it will be necessary to go back, and give an account of the formation of the Order of S. P. K.

At a session of the Provisional Supreme Lodge, held at Washington, D. C., June 8, 1868, P. S. C. Barton offered the following resolution:

"*Resolved*, That notwithstanding any law or order to the contrary, power and privilege is hereby granted the founder of the Order to create and establish a higher degree or degrees, that shall in no wise interfere with the Ritual of the Order, to be entirely different therefrom, and to have its own Grand Lodge, Supreme Lodge, etc."

"Subsequently, at the same session, three thousand copies of this 'Higher Degree' were ordered to be printed."

As to the meaning of this resolution, there has been much discussion. On the one hand, it has been claimed that it does not require that the degrees should be reported to the Supreme Lodge for their approval; that the permission accorded was absolute, without any recourse; that, from the use of the words, "to create" and "to establish," as well as from the fact that it was to have its own Grand and Supreme Lodges, the resolution took all control over the new degrees out of the hands of the Supreme Lodge of the Knights of Pythias.

On the other hand, it is claimed that the founder of the Order (Brother J. H. Rathbone) was only empowered to act as a Committee, as he had in one or two other previous instances, and was to report to the Provisional Supreme Lodge his action ; and the statement that the new degrees were to have their own Grand and Supreme Lodges was only an instruction as to their form.

Within one month after the adoption of this resolution, Damon Conclave, No. 1, Supreme Order Pythian Knighthood, was organized at Washington, composed of members of the various Lodges in the city, with P. S. C. J. H. Rathbone at its head.

At the session of the Supreme Lodge, held at Washington, August 11, 1868, the following resolution was introduced and adopted:

"*Resolved,* That the Supreme Lodge recognize no higher degree or degrees of the Order than those now established in the Ritual of the Order."

In the interim between the passage of this resolution and the adjourned session of the Supreme Lodge, held at Wilmington, Del., on the 9th and 10th of November, 1868, the name was changed from S. O. P. K. to Order of S. P. K. At this session a resolution was introduced and passed, setting forth the action of the previous session of the Supreme Lodge, refusing to recognize any higher degrees, stating that Conclaves had been organized, and that it was the open boast of its members that they received none but Knights of Pythias into their organization, and warning all Brothers against affiliating with "any institution pretending to have any connection with K. of P."

No heed was paid to this warning. Conclaves were organized in the District of Columbia, Maryland, Virginia, Pennsylvania, and New Jersey, the members proclaiming they had nothing to do with the Knights of Pythias.

Thus matters stood at the meeting of the Supreme Lodge, at Richmond, March, 1869. At this meeting the subject of the Conclaves called forth an earnest and lengthy debate, and one that was conducted with much sharpness on both sides. Resolutions were introduced looking to the suspension of all members of the Conclaves who refused to disconnect themselves with that body. The debate, during the forenoon of the second day's proceedings, had become very bitter, when P. G. C. Lowry, of Pennsylvania, moved that the matter be postponed until 3 o'clock, P. M., and that, in the interim, consultation be held with members of the Conclaves, several of whom were members of the Supreme Lodge.

On re-assembling P. G. C. Lowry moved that the whole matter be referred to a Committee of ten, five of them members of the Conclaves, and five not. The vote on the adoption of this measure stood thirty-one to ten. In a short time they returned and submitted the following report:

"That the Rituals of the Order of 'S. P. K.' shall be laid at the altar of the Supreme Lodge, the members of the Supreme Lodge obligating themselves to keep forever secret any of the matters in said Rituals."

Appended to this was the following request:

"The Committee on behalf of the Order of 'S. P. K.,' pray that the Supreme Lodge may adopt the Rituals of the 'S. P. K.' as a side degree of the Order of Knights of Pythias."

The vote on the adoption of the Report of the Committee stood thirty-four to seven. In accordance with this vote the Rituals were placed upon the altar, and the "work" exemplified by P. S. C. Rathbone, and others.

Later in the session, a resolution was passed placing the whole subject in the hands of a Committee of five, clothed with "full power to do and perform all things required to protect the rights, privileges, and prerogatives of all Conclaves, or Brothers connected therewith, and the welfare and interests of the Order of the Knights of Pythias."

Shortly after the close of the session of the Supreme Lodge, the Committee met in Philadelphia, and decided on a plan, of which the following were the main features:

That no new Conclaves shall be organized prior to the second Tuesday of March, 1870.

That no new members be initiated.

That the Conclaves remain as they were, or surrender their Charters, Ritual, etc., to the Committee.

Upon a strict compliance, the Committee will recommend the adoption of the degree of "S. P. K." as an additional degree of the Knights of Pythias.

The Conclaves for the most part refused to submit. P. S. C. Rathbone was at once expelled for surrendering the Rituals, and three jurisdictions at least, those of District of Columbia, Maryland, and Pennsylvania, continued at work. The Charter of the Conclave at Richmond was given up under protest, but subsequently demanded as were the Rituals surrendered by Brother Rathbone, but were not returned. The Conclave at Trenton, N. J., consented to abide by the plan of government until the session of the Supreme Lodge.

At the session of the Supreme Lodge held in New York, March, 1870, the subject was again brought up. A large part of the report of both

the Supreme Chancellor and the Supreme Recording and Corresponding Scribe were taken up with
matters pertaining to the Conclaves. The Committee on Conclaves reported their action, which
report was referred to a special committee, who recommended that the matter be recommitted to the
first, to report some proper resolution.

On the afternoon of the fourth day the matter
was again brought up. The original report of the
Committee was again read, and the additional one,
which they had been instructed to frame, reported.
This called forth a most exciting debate ; amend-
ments and substitutes followed each other in rapid
succession. This state of things lasted until twelve
at night, when the question was settled by the
adoption of an amendment to the report of the
Committee offered by P. G. C. Lowry, which was
further amended by P. G. C. Latham. This, in
effect, suspended all Brothers, members of the Order of "S. P. K.," who refused to furnish evidence
within sixty days, that they had disconnected themselves with the Order. Any Grand or Subordinate
Lodge which refused to obey the mandates of the
Supreme Lodge was to be deprived of its Charter.

At one o'clock, Saturday morning, the Supreme
Lodge went into secret session. It was in this ses-

sion that the O.B.N. was adopted, about which so much has been said and written. Every member who was present subscribed to it, and it was ordered to be administered to every member of the Order, and to all who should thereafter be initiated.

Trouble at once arose ; most of the jurisdictions passed resolutions sustaining the Supreme Lodge, and requiring the enforcement of its mandates in their Subordinates. Several, however, have refused, and in two States at least, Maryland and New Jersey, it has led to the disruption of the Grand Lodges. In Pennsylvania and Maryland the matter has been brought into the civil courts.

In Pennsylvania, G. C. Lowry at first endeavored to have the members of the Lodges in his jurisdiction take the obligation, but he soon saw, or thought he saw, that this was not only illegal, but impossible, and at once recalled his first order, and promulgated the O.B.N. a second time, limiting it to members of the Conclave only. This called forth an order for his suspension from Supreme Chancellor Read. Brother Lowry refused to recognize the order as legal or valid. The case was at once carried to the courts, where a decision was made confirming the Grand Chancellor in his office.

Such is a brief *résumé* of the history of the Conclave and O.B.N. excitement. We have endeavored to give the main features only, and have not entered into details, as these can be found in the Grand and Supreme Lodge Reports.

The further doings of this session of the Supreme Lodge, of importance, were the adoption of a Mariner's Sign, the appointment of a Committee on Flag, some changes in the Ritual, and the voting of an appropriation to extend the Order into Germany and England.

This was by far the most important session held, and has called forth more comment throughout the Order than any other. The wisdom of some measures remains to be seen, while others have already been proven to be harmful to the best interests of the Order.

Chapter XV.

The Order in District of Columbia, Pennsylvania, Maryland, New Jersey, and Delaware, after the organization of the Supreme Lodge.

E have brought our report of the five Grand Lodges that assisted in forming the Supreme Lodge down to the organization of this body. It remains now to follow their history to the present time. We confess the difficulty we have in this attempt. In three of these States, at least, much bitterness has arisen. Ours is a young Order, one without any historic footmarks. Precedents have had to be made and decisions given without hardly any opportunity for thought. So, too much of our legislation has been experimental in its nature rather than final. This is to be expected, and can not well be avoided, the point to guard against is in being unwilling to yield when experience has shown us our error.

So, though there have been differences of opinion, the bonds of Friendship that unite us are far too strong to permit any permanent division, and as we grow older and experience comes to us, though it be sometimes through failures, these little things that trouble us now will be seen in their true proportion, while our glorious principles will so far overtop them that they shall appear very insignificant.

The greatest progress that has been made in any State has been in Pennsylvania. During the year 1869 there had been an increase of one hundred and seven Lodges, the number in the city of Philadelphia being about one hundred, with a larger membership than any other secret or benevolent organization. At the July session of 1869 a Committee was appointed by the Grand Lodge to manufacture paraphernalia. They immediately went to work with that energy that has always characterized the acts of Pennsylvania Knights, and their first report presented at the January session, 1870, showed that they had supplied forty-eight full Lodge outfits and thirty-one partial.

The Knights of Philadelphia early took measures

to provide a suitable place for the burial of the
dead of the Order. At the July session, 1869,
"The Special Committee on Cemetery" submitted
propositions from two parties, with a recommenda-
tion that a committee be appointed to confer with
a Board of Managers, at the head of which stood
S. V. P. Myers. Such a Committee was appointed
with power to act. At the January session this Committee reported, stating that the Cemetery Company
had secured a tract of fifty acres in the Twenty-third
Ward, Philadelphia. This was to be sold in lots to
members of the Order at $15 each, to be paid in
installments. They also agreed to pay to the Grand
Lodge $1 for each lot sold, or $10,000 ; and further-
more to donate five thousand feet to this body, and
one hundred and eighty feet to every Lodge in the
city, "as a place of sepulcher for such poor and in-
digent Brothers, or their widows and orphans," as
the Lodges might have to provide a place of burial
for. The report was accepted and the proposal
agreed to. The Brothers of Philadelphia are to be
congratulated on this achievement. It is an honor
not only to them but to the Order generally. It
shows that our principles are something besides
words ; that what we profess, that we practice.

The year 1870 was not so prosperous as the preceding one. It was early in this year that the action on the O.B.N. was taken that led to the attempted suspension of Grand Chancellor Lowry, and the consequent suits in the civil courts. This deserves more than a passing notice.

In a previous chapter we have given an account of the rise of the Conclaves of the Order of S. P. K., and the circumstances under which the O.B.N. was adopted. G. C. Lowry took a prominent part in the proceedings on the floor of the Supreme Lodge, offering an obligation which was not, however, adopted. On his return to Philadelphia the Grand Chancellor at once, May 1st, promulgated the O.B.N., commanding that it be administered to every member of the Knights of Pythias in Pennsylvania. This Order was met by a perfect storm of refusals ; forty-three out of forty-five thousand Knights in the State refused to take it. The Grand Chancellor became convinced that his Order would not be obeyed, and at once recalled it, and, after consultation with the Grand Officers, issued it a second time, May 20th, limiting it to members of the Conclaves alone.

As a result of this act, having first demanded that the O.B.N. be enforced, and meeting with a refusal, Supreme Chancellor Read suspended the Grand

Chancellor, and appointed the Vice-Chancellor John Stotzer in his stead. On the 8th of June, Brother Lowry issued his proclamation in answer to that of V. G. C., denying the right of the Supreme Chancellor to remove him or suspend him without a trial, and warning all Lodges to receive no documents from any person claiming to be Grand Chancellor other than himself. He also directed that all action on the O.B.N. be suspended until the semi-session of the Grand Lodge, and also that representatives should be admitted to the Grand Lodge without any qualification except that required by the Constitution and laws of the Order.

In reply to this, V. G. C. Stotzer issued a proclamation rehearsing what he claimed to be the facts in the case, and commanding obedience to himself as the legal Grand Chancellor of Pennsylvania.

For a few days matters stood thus, Brother Lowry being sustained by the greater part of the members of the Order in the State, and Brother Stotzer having possession of the office and seal of the Grand Lodge.

On the evening of the 23d of June, G. C. Lowry convened a meeting of the Representatives of the Subordinate Lodges at United Hall, Philadelphia, for the purpose of "advising as to the course to be pursued prior to the semi-annual session of the

Grand Lodge, to provide for the performance of the duties of such of the Grand Officers as refused to acknowedge the legally elected Grand Chancellor." At this meeting a Committee was appointed to take out an injunction against G. V. C. Stotzer, to restrain him from acting as Grand Chancellor, and also another to prepare a protest against the action of the Supreme Chancellor.

The court into which the matter was carried granted the injunction, deciding that the acts of V. G. C. Stotzer were illegal. The Committee to prepare a protest, reported at the beginning of the July session of the Grand Lodge, rehearsing the facts with comments, and closing by submitting a series of resolutions condemning the O. B. N. as unnecessary and illegal, and as *ex post facto*, entering the solemn protest of the Grand Lodge against it, and calling on the Supreme Lodge to reconsider its action and absolve all who had taken the O. B. N. This report was adopted by a vote of one hundred and eighty-four yeas to thirty-three nays. Later in the session two thousand copies of the protest were ordered to be printed.

The sum of $425 was also appropriated to defray the expense of taking out the injunction. Several resolutions were passed, all looking to a repudiation of the O.B.N. Representative Linton, who was strongly in favor of the O.B.N., tendered his resignation rather than vote as he had been instructed to do. This was accepted, with a vote of thanks for his services. A resolution of confidence in G. V. C. Stotzer was also passed, and another directing that those officers who had been installed by his authority be properly installed by the Grand Lodge officers.

The feeling of this session of the Grand Lodge on the matter of the O.B.N. can not be doubted ; it was one of decided and outspoken opposition. As we are writing, the returns for the election for 1871 are coming in, and they seem to indicate that not one candidate who has been in favor of the enforcement of the O.B.N. has been elected to office in the Grand Lodge.

But notwithstanding this difficulty, the year has been very prosperous. We have no data of the number of members, but there are two hundred and eighty-four Lodges in the State, an average increase of one each, week.

The jurisdiction of MARYLAND has been singularly unfortunate, even more so than its sister-jurisdiction, Pennsylvania. . Previous to the session of the Supreme Lodge at Wilmington, trouble had arisen caused by the decease of Grand Chancellor Campbell. The Grand Vice-Chancellor Abbott succeeded him, but for a time his authority was doubted. The Supreme Chancellor, before whom the matter came, decided that G. V. C. Abbott was the rightful Grand Chancellor, and must be obeyed as such.

Some troubles having arisen concerning an alleged illegally called session of the Grand Lodge, the Supreme Chancellor issued an order declaring all the acts of this special session illegal and improper, but at the same time recommended that certain acts be confirmed, among which was the issuing of Charters to two Lodges that had been chartered at this special session. This was done.

The matter of the Conclaves has also caused trouble in Maryland. After the action of the Supreme Lodge.at the session of 1869 concerning this body, it was ordered to be communicated to the Lodges. In the copies of the Report of the Proceedings of the Supreme Lodge sent to the Subordinates, a circular was inclosed stating the action in regard to Conclaves. These were forwarded to the Grand Chancellor of each State, with directions that they be transmitted under seal. This was not done in

19

Maryland. The Grand Chancellor laid them before
the Grand Lodge in special session, and by it they
were laid on the table. This action was reported at
the next session of the Supreme Lodge, 1870. A
resolution was introduced censuring the Grand
Lodge, and directing that the vote of censure be
communicated to them.

This, instead of healing the trouble, only made it
worse. As in Pennsylvania, the Grand Lodge refused to obey the mandates of the Supreme Lodge.
This called forth an order from Supreme Chancellor
Read, charging the Grand Chancellor and Recording and Corresponding Scribe of the Grand Lodge
of Maryland with resisting the Supreme Lodge, declaring them in a state of insubordination, and sus-
pending them from office. G. V. C. Steiner was
appointed Grand Chancellor, and Thomas S. Uppercue Grand Scribe. The Grand Officers refused to
obey the order of Supreme Chancellor Read, and
continued to exercise the functions of their office.
On the 28th of June a special session of the Grand
Lodge was called for the purpose of adjusting these
difficulties. Forty-two Lodges were represented at
this meeting; a resolution was adopted recognizing
the officers whom the Supreme Chancellor had attempted to remove, as the only legitimate officers,

and commanding obedience to them under pain of forfeiture of Charter. There were only two dissenting votes on this. At the same time, the actions of the D. G. C. Bates and of D. G. R. and C. S. Uppercue, the officers appointed by the Supreme Chancellor—they having expressed their willingness to recognize the officers of the Grand Lodge—were legalized so far as any official act was concerned.

This did not allay this trouble. At the semiannual session of the Grand Lodge in July, 1870, the reports show a great amount of insubordination. Lodges refused to allow their officers to be installed except under authority of the Supreme Lodge, and others failed to pay the percentage due the Grand Lodge. A resolution requesting the Supreme Chancellor to call a special session of the Supreme Lodge for the purpose of allaying the difficulties which had arisen from the enforcement of the O.B.N., was passed. It may be said here that this request was refused.

Thus matters stood until the 15th of December, 1870. On this day a Grand Lodge was organized at Baltimore, comprising those Lodges which were in accordance with the Supreme Chancellor. Fifteen Lodges out of the fifty-nine in the State were represented. General Steiner was elected Grand

Chancellor, and Thomas S. Uppercue, Grand Recording and Corresponding Scribe. The old Grand Lodge at once applied to the courts for an injunction restraining Supreme Chancellor Read from forming another Grand Lodge. This application was refused on the ground that the jurisdiction of the Supreme Lodge over the Grand Lodge was only spiritual, and that this was not subject to the civil power unless good morals were set aside, or action taken in violation of the peace and good order of the State.

As matters stand, then, in Maryland, there are two Grand Lodges, both claiming to be legal. This will complicate the settlement of the question at the next session of the Supreme Lodge, and will also bring the matter up early in the session, as there will probably be two delegations present from this State.

Concerning the history of the other of the five States that formed the Supreme Lodge, it is needless to enter into detail. It is about the same story as in Pennsylvania and Maryland. There has trouble arisen from the same source, and there have been as useless endeavors to prevent it. In New Jersey there are two Grand Lodges; one, composed of about forty of the Subordinate Lodges, being in harmony with Supreme Chancellor Read ; the other, comprising the remaining nineteen, refusing to have any thing to do with the O.B.N.

It is in these five jurisdictions that the main trouble has arisen. In most of the other States the Order is new, and during the formative period but little time can be given to such matters. The great aim is to extend the Order.

Chapter XVI.

The Order in New York, Virginia, Connecticut, Louisiana, Nebraska, California, West Virginia.

E realize the difficulty under which we labor in attempting to give an account of the rise and progress of the Order in the various States. Some accounts may seem too full to some, while to others they will appear meager. We have endeavored to avoid detail, and to give those facts that will be of general interest. We have in every case endeavored to learn to whom the Order is indebted for its introduction into each State, and have given the results of our investigations. In some instances we have been unable to gain the desired information. Where the subject has been doubtful, we have chosen that side that seems to be best supported.

222

NEW YORK.

As early as February, 1868, efforts were made by a member of the Grand Lodge of Pennsylvania to introduce the order into the Empire State. For this purpose several letters passed between him and B. F. Diercks and J. H. Schutte, of New York city. Some time in April an agreement was entered into between these two gentlemen, and several other parties, to make all possible effort to organize a Lodge of the Knights of Pythias in the city. In consequence of this promise, which had been repeated to him, G. R. and C. S. Blancbois prevailed upon P. S. C's. Rathbone and Westwood, who were in Philadelphia, to go to New York, and furnished them with letters of introduction to Brother Schutte. On their arrival, May 17th, Brother Schutte accompanied them to many of his friends, and as a result it was agreed to organize the Lodge on the evening of the next day, May 18, 1868.

On this evening the first meeting was held at the old Warren Hall, corner of Oliver and Henry streets, and the Lodge instituted under the name of Rathbone, No. 1, by the two Brothers before named.

The number initiated was only thirteen, but in

eight months it had increased to over eight hundred. At present there are nearly, if not quite, forty Lodges in the State.

On the 14th of October a dispensation was issued to organize a Grand Lodge, in compliance with which the Grand Lodge of New York was instituted October 29, 1868—five Lodges being represented. The first officers were as follows:

Dr. H. W. Good, Grand Venerable Patriarch.
Dr. Abram G. Levy, Grand Chancellor.
William A. Hayward, Grand Vice-Chancellor.
B. F. Diercks, Grand Scribe.
Simon J. Wienthal, Grand Banker.
A. Abrams, Grand Guide.
Jacob Regus, Grand Inside Steward.
C. W. Auffarth, Grand Outside Steward.

Much of the success of the Order in this State is confessedly due to Past Grand Chancellor Dr. A. G. Levy. He and his "partner in business have translated the Ritual into the German and French languages, and are now engaged in translating it into the Spanish." Though the progress made in this State has not been as great as in some others, New York Knights have no reason to be ashamed. They have had difficulties to contend with of which other jurisdictions have no knowledge, but there is a brilliant future before our Empire State brethren.

VIRGINIA.

Of the history of our Order in the Old Dominion we can say but little—not from a want of inclination, but from a lack of information. We have already, in our history of the Grand Lodge of the District of Columbia, given an account of the organization of Alexandria Lodge, No. 1, at Alexandria, and of its subsequent history. This was started through the labor of P. G. C. King, and had an existence of only about three months. The work belonging to this extinct body came into possession of the Grand Lodge of Pennsylvania, and was by it surrendered to the Grand Lodge of Virginia, on a request from that body.

The Order was re-established somewhere about the time of the organization of the Supreme Lodge, through the exertions of P. G. C. Hartman, by the institution of Virginia, No. 2, at Richmond, Va. This was numbered 2, and allowed to remain so for the same reason that Franklin Lodge, of the District of Columbia, still retains its number, though it has long been the first on the roll. The latest information we have at hand (December, 1870) concerning the state of the Order, shows sixteen Lodges in operation, with about two thousand members. (Sprig of Myrtle.)

For a time the Order languished. One Lodge—Hartman, No. 8, Petersburg—ceased work, but latterly a new spirit has been infused into the members. Lodges are multiplying, efforts are being made to resuscitate Hartman, and initiations are frequent.

There is an act recorded of a Knight of Pythias in this jurisdiction, that should be put in such a form as never to be forgotten. It is worthy of the highest encomiums and deserves to be perpetuated for the honor it has thrown upon our principles. We will let Brother John E. Edwards, of the Old Dominion Lodge, No. 4, tell the story.

"Samuel H. Hines merits all that can be said of the moral hero, the brave Knight, the Pythian friend. When the fated Spotswood Hotel was wrapped in the winding-sheet of lurid flame, on the morning of December 25, 1870, and its passages, rooms, and stair-ways were filled with dense clouds of suffocating smoke, Captain Hines made his way through all to a point where he was safe, and might have escaped with his life unharmed. But personal escape from danger was not his object; he was seeking aid to rescue his friend who was high up in the hotel. Failing to enlist assistance, despite remonstrances he rushed back, with the heroic purpose to save that friend, or perish in the effort. This was the last of this noble young man. He and his friend Erasmus W. Ross, a brother Knight, perished together.

"In this notable deed we have embodied and illustrated in living examples a *friendship* unsurpassed by any thing described by the pen of fiction, or depicted in dramatic art. This is no fiction, no poetic fancy, no sentimental creation. Samuel H. Hines did not merely hazard life, but really *died* to save his friend. It is an honor and a privilege to have known such a man, or to have lived in an age made bright by such an example. All honor to the name, the virtues, the friendship, the moral heroism of Samuel H. Hines.

.   .   .   .

"The death of *such* a man is a public calamity. It is not enough for the universal Brotherhood of Knights to appropriate such a distinction for one of its members. Let *humanity* share with us this exalted privilege. Let the world know that Pythias himself did not surpass, in his devotion to Damon, one who lived in our own day, who bowed at our

own altar.   Thank God, it is not all a calamity, not
all a disaster, not all a cause of sorrow, not all an
irreparable loss, when we remember that one of our
own race, of our own flesh and blood, of our common humanity, *can* display—nay, more, *did* display—
such a heroic example as that which was made imperishable amid the charred and blackened ruins of
Spotswood Hotel.   It is well to have lived such a
life; it is nobler to have died such a death."

CONNECTICUT.

This State has shown itself to be a fruitful field
for the growth of Pythian Knighthood.   The first
of the New England States to receive the Order, it
has never been backward in extending it.   It gave
it to Massachusetts; and, though the Bay State has
outstripped it in number of Lodges, in zeal and toil,
it is no way in advance of the "Nutmeg State."

It was in New Haven that the Order first took
root.   Several gentlemen of this city, who were
members of both the Masons and Odd-Fellows,
were initiated into the Knights of Pythias in the
city of New York, by D. G. C. A. G. Levy.   On
their return to Connecticut, they proceeded to make
the necessary arrangements to found a Lodge in

New Haven. The petition was forwarded to the D. G. C. of New York, and by him to the Supreme Chancellor. The dispensation was granted by the Supreme Lodge, in session at Wilmington, and on the 17th of November, 1868, Rathbone Lodge, No. 1, was instituted, with the following officers:

JOHN F. COMSTOCK, Venerable Patriarch.

N. D. FORBES, Worthy Chancellor.

C. B. HINE, Worthy Vice-Chancellor.

GEO. A. STEVENS, Banker.

E. L. BISSELL, Recording Scribe.

C. K. BUSH, Financial Scribe.

J. J. OSBORN, Guide.

F. S. BEECHER, Inner Steward.

G. W. DOUGLASS, Outer Steward.

Edward W. Dawson was appointed D. G. C., and without delay the work of organization of new Lodges progressed. Just one month from the introduction of the Order into the State, Dawson Lodge, No. 2, was instituted at Fair Haven, and six days after, December 23d, Ezel Lodge, No. 3, at New Haven. In less than six weeks after the introduction of the Order into the State, three Lodges had been organized and applications received for two others. The new Society was every-where received with marks of the utmost favor, though whisperings were heard that it was a secret political organization.

Measures were at once taken to organize a Grand Lodge. An application for a dispensation so to do was made out, and forwarded to the officers of the Supreme Lodge. It was promptly granted, and, on the 18th of January, 1869, the Grand Lodge of Connecticut was organized in New Haven, with Edward W. Dawson as Grand Chancellor.

Nowhere in the United States has the Order advanced so rapidly as in Connecticut. It had much to contend with. The conservative ways of its people are well known to those who have resided among them, and the animosity of each political party to any thing that is suspected, even though falsely, of a bearing toward its opponent. Yet the Order has prospered. Thirty-one Lodges are on the Roll, and the membership, in position and influence, may safely challenge that of any other State.

LOUISIANA.

Sixth upon the roll of States into which our Order has been introduced stands Louisiana. Its rapid spread in other jurisdictions has, for some reason, not found its equal in this. It may be that the quarrels of other and older fraternities, which have been very bitter, have made this State an unpromising field for the extension of the Knights of Pythias. As it is, though the first movement toward the establishment of our Order in this State was made January 28, 1868, there is not, as yet, a Grand Lodge organized, but the subordinates are working under direction of the Supreme Lodge.

On the above date, Brother Alfred Shaw, who was at the time in Philadelphia, sent a note to the Grand Recording Scribe of the Grand Lodge of the District of Columbia, which was at that time acting as a Provisional Supreme Lodge, requesting a Charter for a Lodge to be located at New Orleans, where he was then going to reside. This request was not complied with, on the ground that the requisite number of signatures did not accompany the application. That he might have an opportunity, however, to carry out his purpose, he was, by resolution, created a Past Chancellor and Deputy Grand Chancellor of Louisiana, and empowered to obligate and instruct a sufficient number of gentlemen to form a Lodge.

On reaching New Orleans, he found that the name, even, of the Order had never been heard. Nothing dismayed, he began earnestly the work of

organizing a Lodge, and soon awakened an interest
in the hitherto unknown Society. As a result of
his labors Ivanhoe Lodge, No. 1, was opened with
Edward S. Wurzburger as its first Worthy Chan
cellor. At the last session of the Supreme Lodge
there were but five Lodges in the State, but have
since been increased, and now number ten.

Brother Shaw having resigned his position as
D. G. C., W. E. Fitzgerald was appointed to fill the
position.

NEBRASKA.

The honor of introducing the Order into this far-
off territory is due to P. G. C. George H. Crager.
Brother Crager was initiated in Rising Sun Lodge,
of Philadelphia, and immediately on his removal to
Omaha succeeded in establishing Nebraska Lodge,
No. 1, at Omaha City, which was instituted December 3, 1869, by Brother Crager, acting as Deputy Grand Chancellor.

The Lodge at the close of the year had on hand
and invested $337.95, and had besides this expended
$300 in fitting up a Lodge-room, and that in less
than a month.

The Knights of Nebraska had the pleasure of
taking part in the celebration in honor of the com-

pletion of the Pacific Railway, and were highly spoken of by the press.

On the 13th of October, 1869, the Grand Lodge was organized by the Supreme Chancellor, with the following officers:

GEORGE H. CRAGER, Venerable Patriarch.

DAVID CARTER, Grand Chancellor.

JOHN Q. GOSS, Grand Vice-Chancellor.

E. E. FRENCH, Grand Recording and Corresponding Scribe.

T. C. BRUNNER, Grand Banker.

WM. L. WELLS, Grand Guide.

JOHN F. KUHN, Grand Inner Steward.

JOHN TAYLOR, Grand Outside Steward.

Five Lodges were represented, and the utmost enthusiasm prevailed. The present condition of the Order we are unable to state, but from the well-known energy of those at its head it must be flourishing.

CALIFORNIA.

On the 13th of July, 1868, Brother John Stratman was initiated into the Knights of Pythias at Washington, and being on the point of leaving for

20

California, he was named D. G. C. of that State,
and took to the Pacific coast the Rituals and private work necessary to establish the Order there.
Previous to this, however, some time in May, 1868,
S. B. and C. S. Barton met Brother Geo. H. Chard,
of Olive Branch Lodge, Philadelphia, and gave him
instructions as to the method to be pursued in organizing a Lodge.   Later, Brother Chard wrote for
further instructions and the necessary documents.
From these resulted an application, forwarded about
the middle of December, for a dispensation to organize Lodge No. 1, which was afterward named
California.

The dispensation was granted and sent to Brother
Chard, with instructions to consult with Brother
Stratman as D. G. C.   Brother Chard at once wrote
that the D. G. C. had left for New York and would
not return until May, and urged that a delay until
that time would be fatal to the interests of the
Order in the State.

On the 12th of October other parties, ignorant
of the action that had been taken, forwarded a petition to organize Damon Lodge, No. 1.   The Supreme Chancellor, to whom the matter was referred,
directed the appointment of Brother Stratman to be
revoked and Brother Chard to be appointed in his

stead, and also ordered that the dispensations and work be forwarded to him for the two Lodges. This was done, and March 25, 1869, California Lodge, No. 1, the pioneer Lodge of the State, was organized.

Early in September the Order was strong enough to form a Grand Lodge, and on the 5th of that month a preliminary meeting was held at Congress Hall in San Francisco for this purpose. Six Lodges were represented by twenty-eight delegates. The officers elected were:

WILLIAM C. MEAD, Grand Venerable Patriarch.

GEORGE H. CHARD, Grand Chancellor.

DAVID KERR, Grand Vice-Chancellor.

R. W. BARCLAY, Grand Recording and Corresponding Scribe.

GEORGE P. FISHER, Grand Banker.

The Grand Lodge was instituted and the officers installed, September 28, 1869; the number of Lodges had increased to eight. The 1st of January, 1870, there were fifteen Lodges in the State with a membership of twelve hundred and eleven. In the latest issue of the *Sprig of Myrtle*, the number of Lodges is stated at seventeen.

WEST VIRGINIA.

In his report to the Supreme Lodge, session of 1869, Supreme Chancellor Read stated that, " Upon the receipt of a petition, in due form, signed by Charles H. Edgecomb and others, asking for a Lodge of Knights of Pythias, to be located at Martinsburg, to be hailed, 'Washington Lodge, No. 1,'" he has directed a dispensation to be issued, dated March 1, 1869. This was the first action toward forming a Lodge in this State, and was due to the exertions of Brother Edgecomb. The application, signed by fifteen of the prominent citizens of Martinsburg, was forwarded to S. R. and C. S. Barten, sometime the last of February, and by him forwarded to the Supreme Chancellor, who took action as above noted. Upon the organization of this Lodge, Brother Edgecomb was appointed D. G. C.

Lodges increased rapidly in this State. Shortly after the organization of the Lodge at Martinsburg, Lodges at Middleway, Piedmont, Berkley Springs, Newburg, and Wheeling, were instituted in rapid succession. On the 5th of July, 1869, due notice having been given, the Grand Lodge was instituted at Berkeley Springs, by the Supreme Chancellor and Supreme Banker. This was the first of the

Grand bodies instituted by the Supreme Chancellor on his journey to California, a journey in the course of which six Grand Lodges were organized. The first officers were as follows:

REV. WM. GERHARDT, Venerable Grand Patriarch.

CHAS. H. EDGECOMB, Grand Chancellor.

J. HOPE SUTER, Grand Vice-Chancellor.

J. RUFUS SMITH, Grand Recording and Corresponding Scribe.

JNO. F. SMITH, Grand Banker.

JOHN H. MILLER, Grand Scribe.

J. H. M'ATEE, Grand Inner Steward.

HENRY HILLARD, Grand Outer Steward.

Sometime in October, 1869, the Grand Chancellor Edgecomb was suspended by his Lodge for twelve months. Brother Edgecomb appealed, and the case was taken before the Supreme Lodge, where a Committee reported that they found nothing to warrant suspension, and directed that he be reinstated with full honors.

This closes the list of States, twelve, in which Lodges had been planted previous to the session of the Supreme Lodge in March, 1869. Our next chapter will show a still greater increase during the remaining part of 1869 and to March, 1870.

Chapter XVII.

E have brought our history of the introduction of the Order into different States down to the session of the Supreme Lodge at Richmond, 1869. In this chapter we shall give an account of its extension during the Pythian year 1869–70. The first State into which it was introduced was

OHIO.

On the 5th of March a dispensation was made out for Steuben Lodge, No. 1, at Steubenville, in this State. The application for this Charter had been made through the exertions of Supreme Banker Wm. A. Porter, of Philadelphia. Brother Geo. B. Means, to whom we are under obligations for many

238

favors, and to whom we desire to render our thanks, has sent us the following account of this Lodge :

Steuben Lodge, No. 1, the pioneer Lodge of the Order of Knights of Pythias in the State of Ohio, was instituted by dispensation from the Supreme Lodge of the World, on March 22, 1869, by Supreme Chancellor Samuel Read, Mt. Holley, New Jersey, and W. A. Porter, of Philadelphia, Supreme Banker and P. G. C. of Pennsylvania, in the city of Steubenville, county of Jefferson, with thirty-two Charter members. The following were the first officers elected and installed :

THOS. ALDRIDGE, Venerable Patriarch.

JAMES KELLY, Worthy Chancellor.

ROBT. N. THOMPSON, Vice-Chancellor.

GEO. M. ELLIOT, Recording and Corresponding Scribe.

CHARLES BLINN, Financial Scribe.

JOSEPH HALL, Banker.

THOMAS HANNA, Guide.

R. M. MYRES, Inner Steward.

THOMAS ATKINSON, Outer Steward.

On April 1, 1869, a communication was received from Supreme Chancellor Read, in conformity with the authority vested in him, declaring the following

Brothers : George B. Means, David Hall, Thomas Hanna, H. Bingner, as Past Chancellors of Steuben Lodge, No. 1, they having been designated by said Lodge as proper persons to be constituted Past Chancellors, which act entitled them to all the rights and privileges as such.

For nearly two months Steuben Lodge stood solitary and alone. At the session of the Grand Lodge of Odd-Fellows of the United States in Philadelphia several Brothers were present from Cincinnati. Three of these, P. C.'s Manning, Williams, and Armstrong, were one evening visiting at the house of Supreme Banker Wm. A. Porter, and saw on the wall a Knight of Pythias Chart. Their curiosity was excited, and, at the solicitation of Brother Porter, they consented to be initiated. As the Supreme Chancellor was in the city, a dispensation was procured to receive their application, ballot, and confer the degrees the same evening. They also made arrangements to institute a Lodge in the Queen City of the West, and on the 10th of May, Cincinnati Lodge, No. 2, was organized. Seven days after three Lodges were instituted at Columbus, and by the 28th of June three more in Cincinnati. These, with one at Cleveland, assisted in the formation of the Grand Lodge.

This took place July 9, 1869. The Supreme
Chancellor, assisted by G. C. Edgecomb and D. G. C.
Carty, obligated the members and installed the
officers. The following were the officers at the
organization :

HENRY LINDENBERG, Grand Venerable Patriarch.
CHARLES L. RUSSELL, Grand Chancellor.
WM. B. KENNEDY, Grand Vice-Chancellor.
JOS. DOWDALL, Grand Recording and Corre-
    sponding Scribe.
GEO. B. MEANS, Grand Banker.
CHAS. H. BABCOCK, Grand Guide.
E. T. HAINES, Grand Inner Steward.
C. B. RIDGEWAY, Grand Outer Steward.

Brother Dowdall had been the Deputy Grand
Chancellor, but on the organization of the Grand
Lodge refused the office of Grand Chancellor, and
was elected Grand Recording and Corresponding
Scribe. The total membership at the organization
was four hundred and fifty-two. At the January
session of the Grand Lodge there were twenty-one
Lodges represented. The Report showed one thousand four hundred and forty-eight initiations, and a
total membership of one thousand seven hundred
and two.

The year just passed has not been as prosperous as it was expected it would be. The reason has not been a lack of work, but the same that has delayed the progress of the Order in other States. There has been no open outbreak in Ohio, but there has been an under-current of deep feeling, and a determination not to yield obedience to what many good men deemed an illegal act. The present Grand Chancellor, Robert B. Innis, has been a faithful and earnest worker, and is deserving of all credit, but affairs beyond his control have worked against all his endeavors and prevented the spread of the Order.

ILLINOIS.

The history of the introduction of the Knights of Pythias into Illinois is but another illustration of the work Philadelphia has done. The credit of extending the principles of Pythian Knighthood into this State belongs to Brother William J. Tussy, of Adherent Lodge, Philadelphia. Immediately upon his removal to Chicago he began to agitate the formation of a Lodge, and with such effect that on the 16th of April, 1869, he forwarded an application for Welcome Lodge, No. 1. The dispensation asked was granted, and on the 5th of May the Supreme

Chancellor, assisted by Supreme Banker William A. Porter, organized the Lodge. For some reason that progress was not made that should have been ; consequently, on the 30th of August the Supreme Chancellor appointed Colonel John W. Kester D. G. C. for the State. This appointment put new life into the Order. In less than a month Welcome Lodge had more than one hundred and twenty-five members.

Dispensations were rapidly granted for other Lodges, and on the 4th of February, 1870, the Grand Lodge of Illinois was instituted by Supreme Chancellor Read and Supreme Inside Steward Harry Kronheimer, with the following officers :

JOHN W. KESTER, Venerable Grand Patriarch.

HENRY C. BERRY, Grand Chancellor.

F. BUCHMAN, Grand Vice-Chancellor.

A. C. GREENBAUM, Grand Recording and Corresponding Scribe.

M. H. POGSON, Grand Banker.

JOHN G. SPRAGUE, Grand Guide.

M. MOORMAN, Grand Inside Steward.

W. H. BENNETT, Grand Outside Steward.

After the installation, the members of the Grand and Supreme Lodges, with a number of invited

guests, repaired to the Briggs House, where a colla-
tion awaited them. Besides the members of the
Supreme Lodge, some of the highest officers of the
State, both of the Masons and Odd-Fellows, sat
down to the banquet, and thus showed their friendly
feelings for the new Order. It was the elder brother
welcoming the younger to the great family of Fraternities.

At a session of the Grand Lodge, held April 2,
1870, a "Board of Control" was created, who were
empowered to rent a hall in Chicago for a term of
years, and to fit and equip it for the meetings of
the Grand and Subordinate Lodges. This was immediately done, and on the 23d of May a hall, ele-
gant in its appointments, and supplied with every
convenience, was dedicated by the Grand Lodge.
Illinois Knights have every reason to be proud of
this enterprise. It shows that with them Pythian
Knighthood is no ephemeral thing, but one destined to be permanent.

KENTUCKY.

For the introduction of the Order into Kentucky,
the State is indebted to the exertions of Brothers
Alonzo and C. R. Brown. While on a visit to

Philadelphia, in the early part of April, 1869, they received all the degrees in one night, by dispensation, and returned to Louisville determined to make an earnest effort to introduce the Order into Kentucky. The requisite number of names was soon procured, and an application for a Charter forwarded to Supreme Chancellor Read. The request being complied with, on the 7th of May CLAY LODGE, No. 1, Louisville, was instituted by the Supreme Chancellor—thirty-two members being initiated.

The work thus begun was carried on with no lack of interest. On the 25th of June, 1869, a second Lodge was instituted at Louisville, Ky., by D. G. C. Lloyd, who has shown himself an indefatigable worker. By the institution of Uhland Lodge, there being now five Lodges in the State, the Supreme Chancellor ordered that a Grand Lodge be organized. This was done on the 17th of July, 1869, by Supreme Chancellor Read in person. The officers were as follows:

WM. M. NICHOLS, Grand Venerable Patriarch.

H. C. LLOYD, Grand Chancellor.

H. T. MORTEN, Grand Vice-Chancellor.

A. RAMMERS, Grand Banker.

W. A. BORDEN, Grand Recording and Corresponding Scribe.

A. Reutlinger, Grand Guide.

C. R. Aulsebrook, Grand Inner Steward.

J. T. Smith, Grand Outer Steward.

The Order at present (January, 1871) numbers thirteen Lodges, and a fair prospect of an increase. Several cities are about to receive Lodges, and if the Knights of Pythias avoid the rock on which other Orders have grounded, namely, the establishment of Lodges in places not able to support them properly, there is a brilliant future before them. The membership are good and true men, and have withal an earnestness that makes these virtues of value.

December, 1870, the first number of the first Knights of Pythias magazine in the world was issued by members of the Order at Louisville.

The Great West having done thus nobly in its efforts to extend the Order, the East again sent in its petition.

MASSACHUSETTS

Early in May applied for its first Charter. The Provisional Supreme Lodge appointed H. C. M'Coy as Deputy Grand Chancellor for New England. At the 1869 session of the Supreme Lodge this appointment was revoked and P. G. C. Edward W. Dawson appointed in his place. Early in May D. G. C. Dawson forwarded an application for a Charter from Fall River, with fifteen names appended. A dispensation was granted and Dionysius Lodge, No. 1, instituted. Springfield was the second city of the Bay State to receive the Order. The "Hub" had not as yet come into the list. On the 23d of September, however, a dispensation was granted to Brother Stillman B. Pratt to organize Boston Lodge, No. 3. Brother Pratt had been a member of the Order in Philadelphia, and, like a loyal Knight, immediately took measures to extend its principles on his removal to Boston.

The acts of the D. G. C. had not been in every respect satisfactory, but as the appointment had been made by the Supreme Lodge in session, the Supreme Chancellor hesitated to revoke it. He, however, made use of the services of P. G. C. Abbott, of Maryland, who was in Massachusetts, in organizing Lodges. On the 17th day of December the Grand Lodge was organized àt St. John's Hall, Boston. There were seventeen Lodges in the State, sixteen of which were represented by upward of seventy Representatives. S. C. Read, S. V. P. W. H. Myers, S. C. Barton, S. B. Porter,

S. G. Abbott, and G. C. Levy, of New York, assisted in the institution.   The following officers
were installed:

> GEO. W. W. GRAY, Grand Venerable Patriarch.
> WM. B. HAINES, Grand Chancellor.
> H. D. MILLER, Grand Vice-Chancellor.
> A. S. JENNESS, Grand Recording and Corre-
>   sponding Scribe.   ,
> WM. RITCHIE, Grand Banker.
> J. S. FARRINGTON, Grand Guide.
> GEO. POLLARD, Grand Inner Steward.
> D. B. DE WOLF, Grand Outer Steward.

The Order has spread in this State with a rapidity
almost equaling that of the early days of Pennsylvania.   The latest information we have gives the
number of Lodges as forty-six, but as this is some
two months old, it is doubtless much greater now.

INDIANA.

For the following account of the introduction of
the Order into Indiana, we are indebted to Past
Grand Chancellor Charles P. Carty, to whom the
State is much indebted for his active exertions in
behalf of the Order.

"On the 5th of April, 1869, while on a visit to Martinsburg, W. Va., I was induced by my friends to unite myself with Washington Lodge, No. 1, of West Virginia. I, like all true Knights, at once became very much attached to the Order, and on my return home (Indianapolis) immediately proceeded to procure names for a Charter, but found this to be a more difficult task than I expected, as every one seemed to have some suspicion that it was probably a revival of the 'Sons of Malta,' as they had heard nothing of the Order previous to that time.

"I however did not give up the work, and after two months canvassing the city, secured the following names on the application for Marion Lodge, No. 1, K. of P. of the State of Indiana: Charles P. Carty, Warner A. Root, Chas. Mansen, E. E. Fast, Chas. L. Busath, D. C. Bergundthal, Jno. R. Morton, M. L. Seddlemeyer, Chas. A. Holt, George Swain, W. M. Oblemeyer.

"This application was dated June 1, 1869, and forwarded to the Supreme Scribe, at Washington. On the 7th of June I was commissioned by the Supreme Chancellor as Deputy Grand Chancellor for the State of Indiana.

"On the 12th of July, 1869, the Supreme Chancellor, assisted by Grand Chancellor Chas. Edgecomb, organized Marion Lodge, No. 1, K. of P., and installed the following officers:

W. A. Root, Venerable Patriarch.

Chas. P. Carty, Worthy Chancellor.

John R. Morton, Vice-Chancellor.

Geo. Swain, Recording and Corresponding Scribe.

David Shissler, Financial Scribe.

Wm. Oblemeyer, Banker.

George Bourn, Guide.

Chas. A. Holt, Inner Steward.

Chas. L. Busath, Outer Steward.

"On the same day an application was made to the Supreme Chancellor for Olive Branch Lodge, No. 2, K. of P. A dispensation was immediately granted by the Supreme Chancellor, the Lodge organized, and the following officers installed:

A. M'Lane, Venerable Patriarch.

A. R. Miller, Worthy Chancellor.

J. A. Elliott, Vice-Chancellor.

R. P. Daggett, Recording and Corresponding Scribe.

J. B. Ryan, Financial Scribe.

J. H. Smithers, Banker.

J. D. M'Cann, Guide.

George W. Ryan, Inner Steward.

"On the 10th day of August, 1869, I received a petition from Ft. Wayne, Ind., for a dispensation to organize Allen Lodge, No. 3, in that city, and on the 25th of August, 1869, assisted by several of the officers of Nos. 1 and 2, I organized the Lodge and installed the officers. On the same day an application for Damon Lodge, No. 4, was received. On the 8th of September Damon Lodge, No. 4, was instituted. On the same day I organized Humboldt Lodge, No. 5, K. of P. (first German.) On the 12th of October, 1869, I received an application for a dispensation to organize Koerner Lodge, No. 6, (German,) at Indianapolis, and on the same day instituted the Lodge and installed the officers.

"Having a sufficient number of Lodges to organize a Grand Lodge, a petition was duly signed by the Past Chancellors of the State, requesting a dispensation to organize a Grand Lodge, which dispensation was duly granted by the Supreme Chancellor, and, on the 20th day of October, the Past Chancellors of the several Lodges assembled, and the Supreme Chancellor organized the Grand Lodge, Knights of Pythias, of the State of Indiana, the following officers being installed:

CHAS. P. CARTY, Grand Venerable Patriarch.
JOHN CAVEN, Grand Chancellor.

J. L. Brown, Grand Vice-Chancellor.

George H. Swain, Grand Recording and Corresponding Scribe.

Geo. F. Meyer, Grand Banker.

J. B. Ryan, Grand Guide.

W. A. Root, Grand Inner Steward.

Chas. Johns, Grand Outer Steward.

"On the 11th of January, 1870, the Grand Lodge
again met in annual session, and the following officers were elected and installed for the ensuing year:

John B. Stumph, Grand Venerable Patriarch.

John Caven, Grand Chancellor.

John L. Brown, Grand Vice-Chancellor.

Chas. P. Carty, Grand Recording and Corresponding Scribe.

Geo. F. Meyer, Grand Banker.

J. B. Ryan, Grand Guide.

Geo. H. Swain, Grand Inner Steward.

Chas. Johns, Grand Outer Steward.

"On the 1st of February, 1870, I received an application for a dispensation to organize Star Lodge,
No. 7, K. P., in the city of Indianapolis, which dispensation was granted.

"On the 1st day of April, 1870, I received an
application from Richmond, Ind., signed by eighteen

citizens of that place, for a dispensation to organize Cœur De Leon Lodge, No. 8, K. P., at that place, and on the 12th of April, 1870, assisted by G. G. J. B. Ryan and others, I instituted said Lodge. No more dispensations were issued previous to the semi-annual session, held on the 12th of July, 1870.

"On the 17th day of August, 1870, an application was received to grant a dispensation to organize Cambridge Lodge, No. 9, K. P., at Cambridge City. On the 17th day of August the Lodge was organized, and on the 11th and 23d of November Lodges were instituted at Connersville and Franklin.

"The prospect for the Order in this State is very flattering. Lodges will be organized this coming year at a great many different parts of the State. Although we have not been as fast as other States in organizing Lodges, yet we are second to none in material for membership, and Indiana is bound to be a success. Our membership at the end of the year 1870 will probably reach seven or eight hundred, with a fine prospect for doubling it the coming year."

IOWA.

An application for a dispensation to establish Star of the West Lodge, No. 1, was made June 19,

1869, through the efforts of Brother B. F. Pinkerton, late of Tremont Lodge, of Pennsylvania. The dispensation was granted, but, in consequence of the delay of Brother Pinkerton in procuring his card, the Lodge was not organized until September 4th. Supreme Chancellor Read and Deputy Grand Chancellor Kester, of Illinois, were present at the organization and installation. Brother B. F. Pinkerton was appointed Deputy Grand Chancellor of the State. On the 25th of November application for dispensation to organize Evening Star, No. 2, was made and duly granted by the Supreme Chancellor. The Lodge, which is composed exclusively of Bohemians, was organized by Deputy Grand Chancellor Pinkerton on the 10th of December. In January last Deputy Grand Chancellor Pinkerton resigned, and removed to the State of Pennsylvania. The Supreme Chancellor appointed Past Chancellor J. L. Enos, of the Star of the West Lodge, to succeed him.

At the last session of the Supreme Lodge both of these Brothers were created Past Grand Chancellors, for their services.

On the Fourth of July the Grand Lodge of Iowa was organized at Cedar Rapids, with the following officers:

ERIC J. LEECH, of Keokuk, Grand Venerable Patriarch.

JAMES L. ENOS, M. D., of Cedar Rapids, Grand
Chancellor.

E. H. WICKERSHAM, of Keokuk, Grand Vice-Chancellor.

EPHRAIM S. HILL, of Cedar Rapids, Grand Recording and Corresponding Scribe.

PETER C. FRICK, of Cedar Rapids, Grand Banker.

C. FORAICE, Grand Guide.

ROBERT HALL, of Mt. Vernon, Grand Inner Steward.

A. J. REBER, of Mt. Pleasant, Grand Outer Steward.

The Order has not spread in this State as rapidly as in some others, but the material is the very
best, as it could but be in Iowa.

The introduction of the Order into

SOUTH CAROLINA

is the work of Brother John D. O'Leary, a member
of Friendship Lodge, No. 8, of the District of Columbia. On the 5th of July, 1869, he forwarded an
application, with twenty names appended, for a dispensation to organize No. 1. The dispensation was
granted by the Supreme Chancellor, and authority

forwarded to Brother O'Leary to organize the Lodge, which was done on the 11th of August. Brother O'Leary, in forwarding his report of the organization of Palmetto Lodge, No. 1, Charleston, says, "The Lodge promises to become a first-class one, and applications for membership are continually made. I am now engaged in another quarter, and will report progress soon. The Knights of Pythias here will be a success."

This Lodge was not in working order for several months, but on the 25th of July, 1870, it was reorganized by D. G. C. S. B. Palmer, of Georgia. Sometime in September an application was received to organize Salamander Lodge, No. 2, which was granted. The Supreme Chancellor also about this time appointed Brother H. Adolph Cohen, of Charleston, as D. G. C. As yet, there are not enough Lodges to form a Grand Lodge, but if earnest effort will accomplish that end, it will not be long delayed.

The twentieth State on our Roll stands

GEORGIA.

The Order here has made more rapid progress than it has in South Carolina. Through the ex-

ertions of P. C. Sanford B. Palmer, of Hermione
Lodge, No. 13, Georgetown, District of Columbia,
an application was forwarded, September 5, 1869,
to organize Forest City Lodge, Savannah, with
twenty members.

In his accompanying letter, he says : " I am glad
to hear of the success of the Order throughout the
country. I hope to be able to announce to you
within a short time that the State of Georgia has
within its borders as zealous a band of Brothers as
can be found wherever the Knights of Pythias are
known, and that in time Forest City Lodge, No. 1,
of Georgia, shall be the means of planting the
myrtle throughout the length and breadth of the
State." The dispensation was granted on the 9th
of September and forwarded to him. On Friday,
the 24th of the same month, Past Chancellor Palmer, assisted by Brother W. L. Humphries and A. B.
Jones, of No. 21, of Pennsylvania ; C. F. Wiltbank,
of No. 35, of Pennsylvania ; William A. Hampton,
No. 61, Philadelphia, and R. A. Williams, of No.
7, District of Columbia, duly organized the Lodge
and installed its officers, and another State was
added to the long list. Great enthusiasm in relation to the Order was manifested by the warm-
hearted people of Savannah, and steps immediately

taken to form new Lodges. The Supreme Chancellor appointed Brother Palmer Deputy Grand Chancellor of the State.

Application was made for a Charter to organize a Lodge in Augusta, Georgia, and granted on the 7th of December, 1869.

On the 31st of December, Brother Palmer forwarded an application to organize Central City Lodge, No. 3, at Macon. In his letter transmitting the application, Brother Palmer says : " I am doing all I can, and it may be that we shall have a Grand Lodge yet before the session of the Supreme Lodge." The dispensation was granted on the 11th of February. (Supreme Lodge Report, 1870.)

There are not as yet a sufficient number of Lodges in this State to organize a Grand Lodge, but the Deputy Grand Chancellor is hard at work to bring this about.

We quote from the Report of the Supreme Lodge again concerning the Order in

WYOMING TERRITORY.

On the 27th of July, through the influence of George W. Sewell, Past Chancellor of Friendship

Lodge, of the District of Columbia, an application was forwarded from Laramie City, with eighteen signatures. A dispensation was granted to organize Laramie Lodge, No. 1, and forwarded to Brother Sewell. Unfortunately for the movement, Past Chancellor Sewell was called East in consequence of severe illness in his family. After the Rituals, dispensation, etc., had been forwarded to his address, Supreme Chancellor Read, during his trip to the Pacific, arrived in that city, and, after fruitless efforts, the Ritual could not be found nor the applicants—many of them having left Laramie for other parts. The Rituals were, however, afterward found, and forwarded by the Express Company to Deputy Grand Chancellor George H. Crager, at Omaha.

On the 12th of October the Supreme Chancellor, who was then at Omaha, granted a dispensation for No. 1, at Cheyenne, and appointed Henry Simons as D. G. C. This was not organized at once, owing to the absence of the D. G. C. in the East. Its organization was still further delayed by a heavy fire, which destroyed the hall in which they were to meet. The Lodge has since been instituted, and is as yet the only one in the territory. There is a prospect, however, of an increase in their number.

On the 11th of February, 1870, Wm. A. Frye and others forwarded an application for Pioneer Lodge, No. 1, Newmarket,

NEW HAMPSHIRE.

This was the first appearance of the Knights of Pythias in the Granite State. The dispensation was granted, and the Lodge organized by G. C. Wm. B. Haines, of Massachusetts.

Lodges multiplied, so that on the 20th of October, 1870, the Grand Lodge was instituted by S. C. Samuel Read, assisted by P. C. O. W. Young, of Massachusetts, and others ; at this time there were seven Lodges in the State, six of which were represented. The following are the Grand Officers :

MOSES A. PERKINS, of Exeter, Grand Venerable Patriarch.

S. S. DAVIS, of Nashua, Grand Chancellor.

J. T. S. LIBBEY, Dover, Grand Vice-Chancellor.

J. L. Dow, Manchester, Grand Recording and Corresponding Scribe.

S. T. MURRAY, Manchester, Grand Banker.

C. H. TRICKEY, Newmarket, Grand Guide.

F. E. HART, Manchester, Grand Inner Steward.

J. O. DAVIS, Newmarket, Grand Outer Steward.

Considerable business was done, the "work" exemplified, and every thing passed off in perfect harmony. The session closed about 11, P. M.

MISSOURI.

We are indebted to Brother Robert Roth, the energetic Deputy Grand Chancellor of Missouri, for the following account of the introduction of the Order into that State. We wish every Brother to whom we have written had been equally prompt in answering our inquiries—our work would be much fuller in its details. Brother Roth writes as follows:

"In June, 1869, I corresponded with Clarence M. Barton, Sup. C. and R. S., regarding the introduction of the Order into Kansas, and after removing to Kansas City, Missouri, I continued to agitate the cause in this place, but without much success until February, 1870, when I met Brother Oscar Persons, of Excelsior, No. 8, of New York; Brother Thomas C. De Luce, of No. 10, of New York; Brother Samuel Hulme, of Nebraska Lodge, No. 1, of Omaha, Neb., and Brother J. E. Neal, of Damon Lodge, No. 2, of Omaha, Neb.

"We at once prepared to call a meeting, inviting the public to attend for the purpose of organizing

No. 1, of Missouri. The meeting came off at the Office of the Empire Life Insurance Company, on the evening of February 18th—about twenty persons were assembled. Mr. P. L. Cooper was called to the chair, myself elected Secretary *pro tem.*, and Hyatt Sinclair Treasurer *pro tem*. After the purpose of the meeting was stated by the chairman, those present were requested to subscribe their names to the application for a Charter. Some twenty names were put down. A resolution was adopted to hold the application list open until February 22, 1870, and the name of the Lodge was agreed upon to be, 'Kansas City Lodge, No. 1, Knights of Pythias of the State of Missouri.' All the subscribers present contributed toward raising a temporary fund to defray necessary expense, and thus $17 were collected, of which $15 were used as Charter fee. At the same time I was authorized to procure the required paraphernalia for a 'first-class Lodge,' and rent a hall. The application list was forwarded by me on the 22d of February, 1870, with forty-five names.

" The Supreme Lodge being in session at the time in New York, the granting of the dispensation was unusually long delayed, after which another delay was caused by sickness of the family of Brother I.

Q. Goss, of Bellevue, Neb., P. G. C., who had been deputized to open the new Lodge.

" According to instructions from the primary meeting, I procured a 'complete Lodge outfit,' rented a hall, of which rent was to be paid from the 10th of March, 1870, and thus was put to quite a considerable personal expense, as the two dollars in the hands of· the Treasurer were soon exhausted.

" On account of the unusual delay the former enthusiasm of the applicants was reduced to an 'almost entire unconcernedness,' and when I was notified by Brother Goss that he would be in our city on the 5th of May to initiate the new Lodge, I made all possible efforts to have the applicants at the Hall, but not *nine* could be brought together until about ten o'clock in the evening, when we had succeeded in collecting a quorum. Past Grand Chancellor I. Q. Goss then examined the withdrawal cards of the following three Knights, who had appeared out of the five assembled in the former meeting : Samuel Hulme, of Nebraska Lodge, No. 1, Omaha, Neb.; J. E. Neal, of Damon Lodge, No. 2, of Omaha, Neb., and Robert Roth, of Tremont Lodge, No. 128, of Tremont, Penn., after which the following gentlemen were obligated as Pages, Esquires, and Knights : August Weber, Theodore

Stritter, M. H. Card, and Solomon Bartenstein.
Brother Monroe Schmahlfeltd, of Humboldt Lodge,
No. 2, of Chicago, Ill., was then admitted as a vis-
iting member, subsequent to which Past Grand
Chancellor I. Q. Goss acted as Grand Chancellor,
and appointed the following Brothers as Grand
Officers for the evening:

J. E. NEAL, Grand Venerable Patriarch.
ROBERT ROTH, Grand Vice-Chancellor.
M. H. CARD, Grand Recording Scribe.
SOLOMON BARTENSTEIN, Grand Financial Scribe.
AUGUST WEBER, Grand Banker.
WILLIAM SCHMAHLFELDT, Grand Guide.
SAMUEL HULME, Grand Inner Steward.
THEODORE STRITTER, Grand Outer Steward.

"Henry Scheid, and F. A. Taft were initiated as
Pages, proved as Esquires, and raised as Knights.
The election of officers then took place, and the
following officers were installed:

J. E. NEAL, Venerable Patriarch.
ROBERT ROTH, Worthy Chancellor.
SAMUEL HULME, Vice-Chancellor.
M. H. CARD, Recording Scribe.
SOLOMON BARTENSTEIN, Financial Scribe.

August Weber, Banker.

Henry Scheidt, Guide.

Theodore Stritter, Inner Steward.

F. A. Taft, Outer Steward.

"Kansas City Lodge, No. 1, Knights of Pythias, of Missouri, was then declared organized, after which Past Grand Chancellor I. Q. Goss made a few well-adapted remarks, and expressed the hope that Kansas City Lodge, No. 1, would always be *number one* in all its dealings. The Lodge so opened was closed at half-past two o'clock in the morning.

"No. 1 opened under very discouraging circumstances, but is at present a "number one" Lodge, with over eighty members, and ample means. Missouri Lodge, No. 2, was organized on the 7th of May, 1870, at St. Louis, Mo., by Past Grand Chancellor I. Q. Goss, of Bellevue, Neb. A Charter was granted under date of May 2, 1870, to organize Franklin Lodge, No. 3, at Pacific City, Mo., but has as yet not been opened, and, I believe, will not be opened. Humboldt Lodge, No. 4, the first German Lodge of the State, was organized June 30, 1870, in this city by myself, opening with nine Charter members. This Lodge, also, had to overcome a great many obstacles, but represents at the pres-

23

ent time a very prosperous Lodge. Hannibal Lodge, No. 5, was instituted at Hannibal, Mo., in the Fall of 1870, by Past Chancellor Lieutenant G. B. Birch. I am informed that Lodges will soon be organized at the following places: Two in St. Louis, one at Palmyra, Mo., one at Syracuse, Mo., one at Independence, Mo."

This ended the list of Lodges to which dispensations had been granted previous to the session of the Supreme Lodge, March, 1870.

Chapter XVIII.

Progress of the Order in 1870, and Present Condition.

E are drawing near the close of our work; we have traced the progress of our Order from its inception during the dark days of our nation's history to its proud position of the third benevolent society in the country in numbers, and the first in point of rapidity of increase. The 31st of December, 1869, there were four hundred and sixty-five Lodges, and a membership of fifty-four thousand two hundred and eighty-nine—there are now over seven hundred Lodges, with an estimated membership of eighty-four thousand. The Order has been planted in thirty-one States and Territories.

The first State that applied for the Order after the session of the Supreme Lodge, was RHODE

ISLAND. The details of the formation of this Lodge we have not at hand. There are at present but two Lodges in the State.

In the Land of Flowers but little better success has attended the establishment of our Order. Application was made for a Charter from Tallahassee, FLORIDA, on the 17th of March, 1870, through the exertions of D. G. C. S. B. Palmer, of Georgia. The petition received twenty-three signatures. George Damon was appointed D. G. C., and a little later installed its officers. Application has been made for a Lodge at Jacksonville, but whether it has been instituted we have no means of knowing.

The next New England State to apply for dispensation was VERMONT.

Vermont Lodge, No. 1, of Rutland, Vt., was instituted on the 1st of July, 1870, with the following officers:

> G. V. R. WILSON, Venerable Patriarch.
> J. M. OTIS, Worthy Chancellor.
> CHARLES CLARKE, Vice-Chancellor.
> JOHN W. CRAMPTON, Banker.
> W. G. JAMISON, Recording Scribe.
> W. L. DAVIS, Inner Steward.
> A. POLAND, Outer Steward.

The officers and members of Crusader's Lodge, No. 24, of Troy, N. Y., assisted in the formation of this Lodge. D. G. C. J. W. Nesbitt was the installing officer.

From the West still more applications came. The next represented was MINNESOTA.

Minneapolis Lodge, No 1, was organized at Minneapolis on the 11th of July, by S. C. Samuel Read. The following officers were installed:

JACOB H. HEISSER, Venerable Patriarch.

DAVID ROYAL, Worthy Chancellor.

E. A. STEVENS, Vice-Chancellor.

E. P. WELLS, Banker.

H. A. SMITH, Recording Scribe.

A. L. FENLASON, Financial Scribe.

C. H. HOPKINS, Guide.

C. H. WILLIAMS, Inner Steward.

U. L. TANNER, Outer Steward.

Jacob Heisser was appointed Deputy Grand Chancellor of the State, and through his exertions still other Lodges have been instituted.

ALABAMA, the twenty-eighth State for Pythian honors, has already two Lodges, one at Huntsville, which was raised through the instrumentality of some members of Osceola Lodge, No. 5, of Newark, and one at Mobile. The latter was instituted by D. G. C. Fitzgerald, of New Orleans.

Supreme Chancellor Read has appointed T. A. Blackman, of Lee Lodge, No. 2, Mobile, as Deputy Grand Chancellor for the State of Alabama. J. M. M. Drake, of Monte Sano Lodge, No. 1, located at Huntsville, has been appointed District Deputy Grand Chancellor for Northern Alabama.

Still later came NEW BRUNSWICK. Through the influence of George Neatly, Esq., one of the newly-elected Past Grand Chancellors of New York, a preliminary meeting of applicants for a Charter to organize a Knights of Pythias Lodge was held in St. John's.

On Thursday, the 29th of September, the Supreme Scribe received an application for a Charter to establish a Lodge in the City of St. John's, Province of New Brunswick, Dominion of Canada. This was the first application for a Charter to establish a Lodge outside of the United States that the Supreme Chancellor had had the pleasure of acting upon. The application bore the names of twenty young men of the above-named city, prominent among whom was Robert Parkin, editor of the *Warden and Monthly Masonic Record*—which has since been made a Knights of Pythias journal also— who had been instrumental in endeavoring to plant the Pythian banner outside the United States, and whose efforts will be crowned with success.

On Friday evening, October 30th, Supreme Chancellor Read and Past Chancellor Schurz, of New York, organized New Brunswick Lodge, No. 1, of K. of P., at St. John's, New Brunswick, Dominion of Canada. Sixty-three members, including the high sheriff, aldermen, barristers, and prominent citizens of that city, were initiated. The following officers were installed:

W. J. M'CORDICK, Venerable Patriarch.
THOMAS WALKER, M. D., Chancellor.
ANDREW J. STEWART, Vice-Chancellor.
DAVID H. WATERBURY, Recording Scribe.
JAMES MOULSON, Financial Scribe.
JAMES THOMPSON, Banker.
FRED. SANDALL, Guide.
DAVID A. SINCLAIR, Inner Steward.
SAMUEL ARMSTRONG, Outer Steward.

Robert Parkin, Esq., was appointed Deputy Grand Chancellor.

On the 31st of August, WISCONSIN joined the family by the institution of Lodge No. 1, at Milwaukee. G. C. Berry, of Illinois, installed the following officers:

A. T. RIDDLE, Venerable Patriarch.

GEO. R. MILMINE, Worthy Chancellor.

J. F. HUNT, Vice-Chancellor.

S. W. COE, Recording and Corresponding Scribe.

C. H. SNETLAND, Banker.

S. C. CURTISS, Financial Scribe.

C. A. CURTISS, Guide.

F. KOHLE, Inner Steward.

C. H. BINGHAM, Outer Steward.

George R. Milmine, the Worthy Chancellor, was appointed D. G. C. of the State. There are at present seven Lodges in existence in the State, and, doubtless, before the Supreme Lodge meets in April a Grand Lodge will be organized, and its Representatives will be found on the floor of the former body.

The last in the list is the glorious OLD NORTH STATE. Stonewall Lodge, No. 1, of NORTH CAROLINA, was instituted at Wilmington, N. C., on Tuesday evening, November 15, 1870, by S. C. Samuel Read, G. C. William H. Wade, and P. G. C. Henry

Hartman, of Richmond, Va. Eighteen members were initiated, including the officers of the Lodge. The following gentlemen were elected officers :

HENRY C. ORR, Venerable Patriarch.

W. M. POISSON, Worthy Chancellor.

W. A. TOLSON, Vice-Chancellor.

W. H. GERKIN, Recording Scribe.

JAMES W. KING, Financial Scribe.

E. J. KREBS, Banker.

JESSE WILDER, Guide.

W. H. DENT, Inner Steward.

O. P. M'EWEN, Outer Steward.

Attempts are being made to spread the Order into other lands. The Ritual has been translated into German, French, Spanish, Bohemian, and Italian. At the last session of the Supreme Lodge, Supreme Chancellor Read offered the following in his report concerning the Order in GERMANY and ITALY :

"There is a large and very respectable German element connected with the Order. They are anxious to have this noble Order extended to their father-land, that their native country may be blessed by the introduction of the Knights of Pythias from America, the home of their adoption.

"Our Ritual is translated into the German language, and we have many inducements to encourage the enterprise. There are, also, some serious impediments, and perhaps the greatest of these is the want of funds and suitable persons to accomplish the work. The latter, I am persuaded, can be found, and believe the German element amply strong and zealous enough to furnish the material aid required, with the "great idea" of linking their adopted home with their father-land more firmly in the bonds of a "common brotherhood," so beautifully taught in the Ritual of this Order.

"Some time since I received an application from Giovanni Patroni, a native of Florence, Italy, a member and Past Chancellor of Lodge No. —, K. of P., of Pennsylvania, praying to be authorized to establish the Order in his native country. He was attending lectures at the University of Pennsylvania, and expected soon to return home. He was, also, very creditably recommended by his Lodge and the Grand Chancellor of Pennsylvania. Just at this time there are insuperable difficulties in the way, and while I am anxious (as every one should be) that the benign influences of the Order should be extended all over the world, due caution must be observed.

" I am gratified in bearing testimony to the agreeable and instructive interview with this Brother in the presence of the Grand Chancellor of Pennsylvania and Deputy Grand Chancellor Alfred Shaw, of Louisiana, and promised to present the subject before your body at this session. The propriety of translating the Ritual into the Italian language will claim your attention."

An appropriation was made to defray the expenses of its introduction into other countries. Owing to the disturbed state of Europe no further steps have been taken, as yet, but the first opportune moment a move will be made.

It may not be uninteresting to give in detail the progress of our Order from year to year, and the Roll of States into which it has been carried. As the returns are made up to the end of the year, we give them to that time. The returns for 1870 not having been received, we have given an estimate for that year:

December 31, 1864,	3 Lodges	. . .	78 members.
31, 1865,	1 "	. . .	52 "
31, 1866,	4 "	. . .	379 "
31, 1867,	41 "	. . .	6,847 "
31, 1868,	194 "	. .	34,624 ",
31, 1869,	465 "	. . .	54,289 "
31, 1870,	700 "		84,000 "

ROLL OF STATES.

1. District of Columbia.	17. Louisiana.
2. Pennsylvania.	18. Iowa.
3. New Jersey.	19. South Carolina.
4. Maryland.	20. Georgia.
5. Delaware.	21. Wyoming Territory.
6. New York.	22. New Hampshire.
7. Virginia.	23. Missouri.
8. Connecticut.	24. Rhode Island.
9. West Virginia.	25. Florida.
10. Ohio.	26. Vermont.
11. Kentucky.	27. Minnesota.
12. California.	28. Alabama.
13. Nebraska.	29. Wisconsin.
14. Indiana.	30. Canada.
15. Massachusetts.	31. North Carolina.
16. Illinois.	

This closes the list of States into which our Order has spread. It is a glorious Roll, and the end is not yet. Other States are waiting to receive the blessings Pythian Knighthood brings. And it shall not stop here. Far over the waters it is destined to spread. There is an old fable which tells that once the whole world was without the blessing of fire. Men lived rudely in huts and caves. In the Summer life was endurable, but when the Winter came men shivered, and froze, and died. At last the gods in pity sent down fire. Some man, with kindness in his heart, lighted his torch at the heaven-sent fire and went from land to land and left its blessing. The poor, naked, freezing savages as they gathered about and felt its warmth, called down blessing on the head of their benefactor. To every land he went, and every-where blessing followed. The cruel earth became kind, men who were savage and beast-like felt their hearts warm toward their fellows, and at last over the darkened earth a brighter day dawned.

This is a fable, but may we not apply it to the progress of our noble Order? Its fire to warm, not men's cold bodies, but their colder hearts, is heaven-sent. It is from God that Friendship came. It is only from the consciousness of a God, who is our Father as well, that we ever feel kindly to our brother. And with this God-given fire we will go into all lands. We will break in pieces and burn the old idols of Self. We will teach men that there is something better to live for than dollars and cents, and when we have done this then shall our teachings be a power. The cruel earth shall become kind again, and a brighter day for humanity dawn.

And this is not all a vision, not all a dream. Even now men are doing battle for Friendship— ten myriads of as true and leal Knights as ever rode forth to do service for God and the Right, are

fighting bravely. One after another bleeding selfs
are hurled on sacrificial altars, and in the smoke
and flame comes down the answer. Out over the
world is swelling a grander psalm than human ears
ever heard before, a birth-song of united hearts,
and this, more powerful than the fabled Orphic lyre,
shall summon stony hearts to dance along and build
themselves into stately temples. Eighteen hundred
years ago the Divine Man of Judea struck the key-
note, and that melody is taking captive the ravished
souls of men. It is flowing now through the hearts
of men in its rich symphonies and glorious modula-
tions. A little while, and in a glorious burst of
harmony, thrilling like the voice of the waters, shall
swell the song that to-night about our Pythian
altars we sing.

Chapter XIX.

Our Principles.

E have finished our task proper, but it may not be out of place to say a few words concerning our principles. This work may fall into the hands of some good and true man, some one who loves humanity and is striving to serve it. To such a one we are willing, as a Society, to extend our hand and bid you welcome to our number and to the great work we have before us. For are you not a brother? Does not this same love for the race inspire us both? Is there not in our hearts the same glorious hope of a peaceful day for humanity? Are we not looking beyond that pest-cloud that is raining down its poison on the world, for the rifted cloud and the beaming sun, and God's bow of promise? And with these glorious aims and grand visions shared in common, are we not brothers by a closer tie than that of a common mother and a common blood? We speak earnestly to you, for we need just such as you to aid us, and you need just the help we can bring to make your efforts most fruitful. One man alone can do much for his fellow, but two together can do vastly more than both alone. This is ever true, but how much more so when there is such an object before us to inspire us! If that stern, truthful father of the Church could declare that God and he made a majority, what would have been the power had he and thousands of men been banded together with God!

But we do not expect you to join with us unless we give you good reasons for such a course, and this we think we can do. We think that we have, in a simple showing of the principles of our Order, an argument that should lead every true man to beat upon our door and demand admittance. And this word demand we use advisedly, for every such man has a right inside our portals and a claim for a place about our altar that can not be gainsayed, and that place he has a right to demand.

First, as to our form. We are a Secret Society. Not secret in the sense that we have any principles we wish or would keep from the world, but secret that we may better perform the mission there is before us. Our principles, our objects, our aims, we freely publish to the world. We strive to impress on the minds of each one who enters our doors these principles and objects in such a way that they never will be forgotten. This we do by certain symbols and symbolic acts. These, together with our means of recognition, are the only secrets we have.

But it is just here that much of the opposition to our Society, as well as to all Secret Societies, begins. "What is the use, of all these symbols?" is asked. "Why not, if you have any thing true to say, why not speak it out at once in words?" For the simple reason that we can not, nor can you. Words fail to express the soul's deepest and truest thoughts. Language can not prison our holiest emotions. It can utter, at best, only what is finite and limited, but symbols body forth the Infinite and everlasting. Indeed, they are the speech of God. If you be a Christian who brings this objection, you are the last one who should ever utter, though it is among this class that we find the most strenuous opposers of symbolic teaching. Let me reason this matter with you as one who knows both sides

24

whereof he speaks. We go back to that night in which He was betrayed, and read the story of that betrayal. It is grand, sublime, touching, and moves us to pity. But tell me, honestly, are you not more touched and more moved as you come to the Eucharistic feast, and often with streaming eyes and quivering lips eat the bread and drink the wine, *symbols* all of His broken body and His spilled blood, and with this before you, dare you say another word about men teaching by symbols? If you do, we know not how to reach you.

But you may not be a Christian, and thus not be able to appreciate the force of this argument. For you we must take another line, and, as Carlyle has argued this eloquently, we quote his words. We refer to his chapter on Symbols, in his peculiar "Sartor Resartus." He says:

"Bees will not work except in darkness; thought will not work except in silence: neither will virtue work except in secrecy. Let not thy right hand know what thy left hand doeth! Neither shalt thou prate even to thy own heart of 'those secrets known to all.' Is not Shame the soil of all Virtue, of all good manners and good morals? Like other plants, Virtue will not grow unless its root be hidden, buried from the eye of the sun. Let the sun shine on it, nay, do but look at it privily thyself, the root withers, and no flower will glad thee. O, my Friends, when we view the fair clustering flowers that over-wreathe, for example, the Marriage-bower, and encircle man's life with the fragrance and hues of Heaven, what hand will not smite the foul plunderer that grubs them up by the roots, and, with grinning, grunting satisfaction, shows us the dung they flourish in! Men speak much of the Printing-Press with its Newspapers: *du Himmel!* what are these to Clothes and the Tailor's Goose?

"Of kin to the so incalculable influences of Concealment, and connected with still greater things, is the wondrous agency of *Symbols*. In a Symbol there is concealment and yet revelation: here, therefore, by Silence and by Speech acting together, comes a doubled significance. And if both the Speech be itself high, and the Silence fit and noble, how expressive will their union be! Thus in many a painted Device, or simple Seal-emblem, the commonest Truth stands out to us proclaimed with quite new emphasis.

"For it is here that Fantasy with her mystic wonder-land plays into the small prose domain of Sense, and becomes incorporated therewith. In the Symbol proper, what we can call a Symbol, there

is ever, more or less distinctly and directly, some
embodiment and revelation of the Infinite; the Infinite is made to blend itself with the Finite, to
stand visible, and, as it were, attainable there.   By
Symbols, accordingly, is man guided and commanded, made happy, made wretched.   He every-
where finds himself encompassed with Symbols,
recognized as such or not recognized: the Universe
is but one vast Symbol of God; nay, if thou wilt
have it, what is man himself but a Symbol of God;
is not all that he does symbolical; a revelation to
Sense of the mystic God-given Force that is in him;
a 'Gospel of Freedom,' which he, the 'Messias of
Nature,' preaches, as he can, by act and word?   Not
a Hut he builds but is the visible embodiment of
a Thought; but bears visible record of invisible
things; but is, in the transcendental sense, symbolical as well as real."

.   .   .   .

"Yes, Friends," elsewhere observes the Professor,
"not our Logical, Mensurative faculty, but our Im-
aginative one is King over us; I might say, Priest
and Prophet, to lead us heavenward; or Magician
and Wizard, to lead us hellward.   Nay, even for the
basest Sensualist, what is Sense but the implement
of Fantasy; the vessel it drinks out of?   Ever in

the dullest existence, there is a sheen either of Inspiration or Madness (thou partly hast it in thy choice, which of the two) that gleams in from the circumambient Eternity, and colors with its own hues our little islet of Time. The Understanding is indeed thy window, too clear thou canst not make it; but Fantasy is thy eye, with its color-giving retina, healthy or diseased. Have not I myself known five hundred living soldiers sabered into crows' meat, for a piece of glazed cotton which they called their Flag; which, had you sold it in any market-cross, would not have brought above three groschen? Did not the whole Hungarian Nation rise, like some tumultuous moon-stirred Atlantic, when Kaiser Joseph pocketed their Iron Crown; an implement, as was sagaciously observed, in size and commercial value, little differing from a horseshoe? It is in and through *Symbols* that man, consciously or unconsciously, lives, works, and has his being: those ages, moreover, are accounted the noblest which can the best recognize symbolical worth, and prize it the highest. For is not a Symbol ever, to him who has eyes for it, some dimmer or clearer revelation of the Godlike?

"Of Symbols, however, I remark farther, that they have both an extrinsic and intrinsic value—oftenest the former only. What, for instance, was in that clouted Shoe, which the Peasants bore aloft with them as ensign in their *Bauernkrieg* (Peasants' War) ? Or in the Wallet-and-Staff round which the Netherland *Gueux*, glorying in that nickname of Beggars, heroically rallied and prevailed, though against King Philip himself? Intrinsic significance these had none—only extrinsic ; as the accidental Standards of multitudes, more or less sacredly uniting together ; in which union itself, as above noted, there is ever something mystical and borrowing of the Godlike. Under a like category, too, stand, or stood, the stupidest heraldic Coats-of-arms ; military Banners every-where ; and generally all national or other sectarian Costumes and Customs ; they have no intrinsic, necessary divineness, or even worth, but have acquired an extrinsic one. Nevertheless, through all these there glimmers something of a Divine Idea ; as through military Banners themselves, the Divine Idea of Duty, of heroic Daring ; in some instances, of Freedom, of Right. Nay, the highest ensign that man ever met and embraced under, the Cross itself, had no meaning save an accidental extrinsic one.

"Another matter it is, however, when your Symbol has intrinsic meaning, and is, of itself, *fit* that men should unite round it. Let but the Godlike manifest itself to Sense ; let but Eternity look, more or less visibly, through the Time-Figure (*Zeitbild*) ! Then is it fit that men unite there, and worship together before such Symbol, and so, from day to day, and from age to age, superadd to it new divineness.

"Of this latter sort are all true Works of Art. In them—if thou know a Work of Art from a Daub of artifice — wilt thou discern Eternity looking through Time ; the Godlike rendered visible. Here, too, may an extrinsic value gradually superadd itself; thus certain *Iliads*, and the like, have, in three thousand years, attained quite new significance. But nobler than all in this kind are the Lives of heroic, God-inspired men; for what other Work of Art is so divine? In Death, too, in the Death of the Just, as the last perfection of a Work of Art, may we not discern symbolic meaning? In that divinely transfigured Sleep, as of Victory, resting over the beloved face which now knows thee no more, read—if thou canst, for tears—the confluence of Time with Eternity, and some gleam of the latter peering through.

"Highest of all Symbols are those wherein the Artist or Poet has risen into prophet, and all men can recognize a present God, and worship the same : I mean religious Symbols. Various enough have been such religious Symbols—what we call *Religious*—as men stood in this stage of culture or the other, and could worse or better body forth the God-like—some Symbols with a transient intrinsic worth, many with only an extrinsic. If thou ask to what height man has carried it in this matter, look on our divinest Symbol—on Jesus of Nazareth, and his Life, and his Biography, and what followed therefrom. Higher has the human Thought not yet reached ; this is Christianity and Christendom ; a Symbol of quite perennial, infinite character, whose significance will ever demand to be anew inquired into, and anew made manifest."

To these words of Carlyle we can add little. They are words that you will not gain their full meaning at once. We can only say on this matter of symbolic teaching that, while you and I are men, and until that time comes that we see eye to eye, we will be unable to do without symbols.

Having thus met this objection, we speak of our principles. The first and foremost, and all-embracing one, is FRIENDSHIP.

As we have stated in the course of our work, it was the beautiful story of Damon and Pythias that first inspired our Founder to write the degrees. This being so, the strongest lesson taught could scarcely

fail to be a lesson of Friendship. The great evil
of the present day is its intense selfishness. The
great want is a state of things that will enable man
to go with confidence to his fellow and trust him
implicitly. We own that such a consummation, de-
voutly as it is to be wished for, will be a thing
difficult to bring about, and yet we claim that we,
as true Knights, are helping to hasten the day.
Somehow—whether originally or by teaching we
will not say—men's souls have become grasping.
These natures of ours are infinite, and as such can
be satisfied only by what is infinite, and that means
every thing. Our souls, had they power, each one
of them would take to itself all the boundless universe. With millions just such souls, each striving
for its infinite portion, there can but be wars, and
strifes, and deaths, and the only way to avoid this
is to teach these souls to be generous, to be
friendly, in true friendship to yield to its brother
part of that which it claims. This we strive to
teach men to do. We endeavor not only to tell
men the beauty and grandeur there is in yielding
their wishes to another, but we strive to tell them
that even their life must not be counted in contrast
with Friendship.

This, alas! is not the way of the world. There

is too little faith in each other, too little belief in exalted and disinterested friendship. There is too little fraternal sympathy, and too little of that love for man as man, for man deprived of all external shows and formulas. We own that love to another can not be furnished to order. Love is not our servant, to whom we can say, " do this, and he doeth it," but he is our master, who sendeth us where he listeth, and yet, as we gather about our altars and by our beautiful Ritual show to one after another that such love is not only possible, but that it has actually existed, men can but be moved by it, and can but pattern after the example given them.

But perhaps you stop me just here and tell me that this is the work of the Christian Church, that their special mission is to teach men this love. If you mean by this that this work is to be confined solely to what is generally known as the Church, that is, the various sects, as the Baptists, and Methodists, and Episcopalians, and Romanists, I deny your position and dare you to the proofs. No body of men has any right to arrogate to itself the privilege of aiding the Great All-Father in bringing his children to love each other. But if you mean that this should be one and is one of the great duties of the Christian Church, I grant it, though as a Christian I am painfully conscious that we are not doing our duty. It is a shame and disgrace to our holy Christianity that this state of things exists.

To put this matter in a practical form. I am a member of one of the Churches of our country, and have the means by documents of proving this; I am also a Knight of Pythias; I am in some distant city, without home or friends and out of money, and am suddenly taken sick. I send for a member of my Church, and at the same time for a brother Knight; which would reach my bedside first and which stay the longest? Would it be the Church, or the Order, that would be found at my bedside oftenest? And if I should die, which would it be that would follow me to the grave? I have no wish to answer these questions, but I know, and you who are reading this know, which it would be, and there can no excuse be made. And now let me ask again, "If we as Knights of Pythias are carrying out the holiest and best duties of humanity, where is the man who loves his race and reverences his God that dare bid us stop?"

A few words more and we are done, and these we wish to say to those who like us bow about our

Pythian altar and own themselves bound by the same ties. There are some things in this earth that were never born to die ; some things that are old as time and yet young as this last morning's day-break. Foremost among these stand the true words and acts of a true earnest man. The rapt prophetic utterances of an unkempt Isaiah, the barbaric war-song of a Deborah and a Barak, the glorious sphere-songs of a Shepherd King, have lasted now these many centuries of time. What an ado we have made through two thousand years about Thermopylæ and Salamis! Why is this? There was some-thing in them that was true. Not true for the age alone, for often they were opposed to the age, but something that was true forever.

And with this as an element of stability let me ask, what is the prospect before us? Is there not something in our principles that is true forever? and if there is, shall we not be recreant to the trust confided in us if for any reason we fail to make our Order what it should be, the greatest, the grandest, the most glorious of the great brotherhood of Fraternities. We go nearer to the human heart than any other, we get nearer the masses, and it is to them we must go if we would be a power in the world. It is in humble cradles that reformers are rocked; it is unknown mothers that fondle the world's greatest men; it is from mangers, and peasants' huts, and monasteries that the leaders of men come. Heaven help us when we strive for honor and riches! Our day is ended. But while we toil to exalt humanity, while we go to the commonalty of mankind, while, in a word, we are faithful and true men, ever in the foremost rank of the great benevolent institutions of the land shall march the KNIGHTS OF PYTHIAS.

APPENDIX.

———————•———————

E have several times, in the course of our work, spoken of the rapid increase of our Order, as compared with other Orders or Fraternities of a similar character. It may not be uninteresting to show by statistics the truth of this statement. For this purpose we propose—in no invidious spirit—to compare ourselves with the Masons and Odd-Fellows. This will be an easy task as far as the latter are concerned, from the fact that they have a Grand Lodge of the United States, where the statistics for the entire land are collated ; but the Masons having no such body it is difficult to give their exact membership. We shall be obliged, therefore, to estimate the strength of the Masonic Fraternity. We can not give in detail the reasons for our estimates, but they can not vary much from the truth.

First, as to MASONRY: Though this Fraternity was probably first introduced into the United States in 1729, its history can not be said to begin until 1733, with the establishment of a Lodge in Boston. It has thus had a life of 138 years. In 1860 there were about 250,000 members in good standing. Our civil war gave an immense impulse to initiations, so that on January 1, 1870, there were about 500,000 Masons in the country. The number of initiations for 1869 was 46,847, though the average had been about 50,000 for several years. The average yearly increase was thus about ten per cent. for the ten years.

ODD-FELLOWSHIP celebrated its semi-centennial in this country in 1869. But, though its existence began in 1819, its real life and energy commenced in 1830. In 1859 there were 234,252 members; in 1869, 268,608—a gain of 34,356, or about one and one-half per cent. per year. During the year ending June 30, 1869, there were 41,183 initiations, and a gain in other ways of 10,744, making a total gain of 51,937. There was a loss at the same time of 26,562, making a net gain of only 25,375, and this on a membership of 243,233.

Let us now compare these figures with the statistics of the KNIGHTS OF PYTHIAS. Though our Order was founded in 1864, it was from 1865 that our success can be dated. We have already given, page 275, the table of increase. This shows of itself all that we can say. In the year 1868 our increase was nearly six hundred per cent.; in 1869, about sixty-six; and 1870, about the same. And it is to be remembered that ours is a new Society. There have been no hundreds of thousands to speak in our behalf, and bring members to our altars, but only a few thousands; and yet we show a record of increase such as no other secret organization can boast.

THE END

Knights of Pythias' Publications

OF

J. HALE POWERS & CO.

DAMON AND PYTHIAS.—Simultaneously with this Third Edition of the Knights of Pythias' History, we present to the Fraternity our new and beautiful *Half-Chromo*, entitled, "DAMON AND PYTHIAS"—a rare gem of art, that can not fail to be appreciated wherever our Order is known and loved. Believing, as we do, that works of art are public educators, and that those who introduce them to the homes of the people are public benefactors, we can not too earnestly call the attention of all true Knights to this charming picture.

In the center are splendid ideal portraits of Damon and Pythias in medallion, while from the accompanying vignettes, representing the "Scene before the Senate-chamber," "Magnanimous Offer of Pythias," "Prison Scene," "Parting of Damon from his Family," and the ever-memorable "Scaffold Scene," one may read the whole story of that "faithfulness unto death" so nobly exemplified by the heroic knight who gave name to our Order. The stately Grecian columns, the statue of "Fidelitas," the arms of Grecian warfare, the twining myrtle, and the emblems suggesting to the initiate what may not be expressed, are all delineated with striking and artistic effect. Receiving at the outset the warmest commendations from the highest authority in the Order, and heartily indorsed by its leading journals, we shall hope soon to see this work in the homes of thousands throughout the land.

Size, 19x24 Inches. Retail price, $2.00.

CERTIFICATE OF MEMBERSHIP.—In response to the numerous inquiries we are daily receiving for a "Diploma" of the Order, that shall be both *artistic* and *correct*, we have, by process of transfer, issued the foregoing picture in another form, introducing a

"Certificate of Membership" in place of the portraits of Damon and Pythias in the center. It is beyond question the finest Diploma ever issued in the interest of the Order, and it comes within the means of every Knight.

Size, 19x24 Inches. Retail price, $2.00.

KNIGHTS OF PYTHIAS' CHART—A beautiful Half-Chromo, worthy of our noble and growing Order, and illustrative of its beautiful teachings. The design is chaste, graceful, and unique, corresponding in architecture, landscape, and ornamentation with Syracuse in the age of Damon and Pythias. It has received the highest praise from Supreme Chancellor Read, Supreme Recording and Corresponding Scribe Barton, and scores of Grand Chancellors and others. It is the "Chart of the Order," selling by hundreds.

Size, 19x24 Inches. Retail price, $2.00.

For these works we want *live Agents*, to *canvass every Lodge in the country*. We first assign a *single Lodge* on trial, but so soon as an Agent has proved himself, *several Lodges*, and promise constant employment.

Canvassing can not be done in the Lodge-room, and we wish no Brother to apply for an agency who will not thoroughly perform the work assigned him, by seeing each member of the Lodge personally, and, if possible, at his home.

☞ Members of all Benevolent Orders will please notice that we make Fraternity Works a specialty, no other firm approaching us in the extent, variety, and excellence of our publications. Our new and beautiful Masonic and Odd-Fellows' Pictures are selling by *thousands*.

To active and persevering Agents we offer on our pictures inducements that are unrivaled, and a commission larger than any other house does or can offer.   Address,

J. HALE POWERS & CO., Fraternity Publishers,
CINCINNATI, OHIO.

www.ingramcontent.com/pod-product-compliance
Lightning Source LLC
Chambersburg PA
CBHW021615270326
41931CB00008B/706